HOUSE OF COMMONS   SES

COMMITTEE OF
PUBLIC ACCOUNTS

Sixty-Sixth Report

MANAGING THE MILLENNIUM THREAT

Together with the Proceedings of the Committee relating
to the Report, the Minutes of Evidence, and Appendices

Ordered by The House of Commons *to be printed*
27 July 1998

LONDON: THE STATIONERY OFFICE
£8·00

816

The Committee of Public Accounts is appointed under Standing Order No. 148 viz:

Committee of Public Accounts

148.– (1) There shall be a select committee to be called the Committee of Public Accounts for the examination of the accounts showing the appropriation of the sums granted by Parliament to meet the public expenditure, and of such other accounts laid before Parliament as the committee may think fit, to consist of not more than fifteen Members, of whom four shall be a quorum. The Committee shall have the power to send for persons, papers and records, to report from time to time, and to adjourn from place to place.

(2) Unless the House otherwise orders, each Member nominated to the committee shall continue to be a member of it for the remainder of the Parliament.

(3) The committee shall have power to communicate to any committee appointed under Standing Order No. 152 (Select committees related to government departments) such evidence as it may have received from the National Audit Office (having been agreed between the Office and the government department or departments concerned) but which has not been reported to the House.

28th October 1997

Ordered, That Standing Order No. 148 (Committee of Public Accounts) be amended, in line 7 [line 4 of this text], by leaving out the word "fifteen" and inserting the word "sixteen".

The following is a list of Members of the Committee at its nomination on 25 July 1997. The date of any later nomination, discharge or other change is shown in brackets.

Rt Hon David Davis (elected Chairman 30 July 1997)
Mr Alan Campbell
Mr Geoffrey Clifton-Brown
Mr Ian Davidson
Mr Geraint Davies
Ms Maria Eagle
Ms Jane Griffiths
Mr Phil Hope
Mr Christopher Leslie
Mr Andrew Love
Rt Hon Robert Maclennan
Ms Dawn Primarolo (added 30.10.97)
Mr Richard Page
Mr Charles Wardle
Mr Dafydd Wigley (discharged 16.12.97)
Rt Hon Alan Williams

The cost of printing and publishing this Report is estimated by The Stationery Office Limited at £1,940.

TABLE OF CONTENTS

Page

SIXTY-SIXTH REPORT

EVIDENCE (*Monday 15 June 1998*) (HC 816-i (97–98))

WITNESSES

APPENDICES

SIXTY-SIXTH REPORT

The Committee of Public Accounts has agreed to the following Report:—

MANAGING THE MILLENNIUM THREAT

INTRODUCTION AND SUMMARY OF CONCLUSIONS AND RECOMMENDATIONS

1. To save memory space, many computer programmers in the past referred to years by their last two digits rather than by all four, 98 rather that 1998; and as a consequence some computers now cannot tell the year 2000 and the year 1900 apart. This could mean that some computers and electronic equipment will produce meaningless information or fail completely.

2. The potential impact is serious: there are few, if any, areas of modern life that are not touched by IT. Even if an organisation's own internal systems and equipment are year 2000 compliant, they might still be unable to continue functioning if others in the supply chain fail. Failures in transports systems, such as air or rail, or utilities, such as electricity, gas or water, could have serious consequences for whole populations. And failures in equipment, such as medical equipment could be life threatening.

3. Estimates of the costs of remedying the problem in the United Kingdom vary quite widely. But the Prime Minister has concluded that estimates which put the cost to the public sector at up to £3 billion are reasonable.

4. The responsibility for ensuring that government business continues without disruption in the year 2000 rests with each government department and agency.   At the centre the Office of Public Service have a monitoring, advisory and co-ordination role, which since 30 March 1998 has extended across the whole public sector.[1]

5. On the basis of a report by the Comptroller and Auditor General, the Committee examined progress in tackling the Year 2000 threat across central government and the wider public sector, and within the National Health Service.[2]

6. In the light of this examination, our over-riding concerns are:

- **Readiness of the wider public sector**

    There is now less than one and a half years before the Year 2000 and many computer systems and electronic equipment may start to fail well before then. There are already signs of slippage in programmes to deal with the problem; costs are rising; and central monitoring of the wider public sector, including local authorities and non-departmental public bodies, has only just begun. The Office of Public Service therefore need to:

    - Ensure that business critical systems, including those that impact directly on citizens and patients, are tackled first;

    - Monitor progress closely, and take or encourage direct action where progress is too slow, especially on those systems critical to public business and to public services;

    - Ensure that contingency plans are in place, and are tested.

- **Readiness of the NHS**

    The NHS got off to a late start in tackling the year 2000 issue, particularly in identifying the potential problems with medical equipment. While the NHS Executive assured us

---

[1] C&AG's report, (HC 724 of 1997–98), para 3.9
[2] ibid

that systems will either be ready, or contingency plans will be in place, they could not guarantee patient safety. They now need to:

- ▸ Take strong and decisive action to ensure that all NHS organisations and GPs are fully prepared;

- ▸ Monitor the position on medical equipment closely, and take every possible step to ensure the safety of patients;

- ▸ Ensure that lack of resources does not result in the failure of systems and equipment that are critical to NHS services and patient care.

7. Our more specific conclusions and recommendations, which underpin these general concerns are as follows:-

On the progress made across central government and the wider public sector

(i) Progress reports for central government already show some slippage and some Departments do not now expect to complete their work until the second half of 1999. As a result, we cannot be sure that government business will not be disrupted in the Year 2000, and in some cases there is little room for manoeuvre if things go wrong. The Office of Public Service need to direct particular attention to those central government departments that do not expect to complete their work until the second half of 1999. (paragraph 27).

(ii) We are concerned that the estimated cost to central government bodies rose by 9 per cent between November 1997 and June 1998. However we note the view of the Office of Public Services that although costs may rise above the latest estimate of £402 million, they should not rise as rapidly as in the past (paragraph 28).

(iii) We note the Office of Public Service's view that the £400 million required by central government can be found from within existing budgets, partly by rescheduling replacement programmes, without any further impact on services. And we are encouraged by the assurance from Treasury that if costs cannot be absorbed by departments they would react sensibly. We expect the Office of Public Services to draw the attention of Treasury to any areas where resource constraints put timely completion of the programme at risk. (paragraph 29).

(iv) We are disappointed that the first attempt to monitor progress across the wider public sector was in June 1998, some one and a half years after the programme began. This has prevented the Office of Public Service from undertaking a comprehensive risk assessment. In the absence of such an assessment, and in view of the patchy returns received so far, we are concerned about the readiness of the wider public sector to cope with the Year 2000 issue and about whether resources are being targeted on those business critical systems most at risk. We expect the Office of Public Service to complete a full risk assessment across the whole of the public sector by mid-1998, to identify bodies and key risk areas that should be targeted for action or intensive monitoring (paragraph 30).

(v) It is not possible to predict the full impact of the millennium threat within an organisation or through the supply chain. We are concerned, therefore, that only half of government departments and agencies have updated their business continuity plans to deal with the year 2000, and that those that exist vary in scope and detail. We look to the Office of Public Service to require all public bodies to have comprehensive, robust business continuity plans in place by January 1999 (paragraph 31).

(vi) We recognise that many of the systems and equipment that need to be replaced or modified were installed well before the scale of the Year 2000 issue became apparent. Nevertheless, we are disappointed that the Office of Public Service has not given a stronger lead on the issue of supplier liability. We expect them to provide guidance and support to departments, agencies and the wider public sector to ensure that wherever possible suppliers that fail to meet their obligations meet the costs involved (paragraph 32).

On the progress made in the NHS

(vii) In view of the potential impact of the year 2000 issue on NHS services and on patients, we are astonished that the NHS Executive got off to such a slow start in addressing the problem. The failure to set deadlines for action in September 1996 was a missed opportunity to ensure that all NHS bodies took the threat seriously. The action taken by the Executive subsequently means that they now have in place the elements of a well managed project (paragraph 50).

(viii) We note that the NHS Executive are confident that all IT systems will be modified in time, and that medical equipment will either be modified or replaced where required. But we are concerned that the deadline of September 1999 for finally checking that all parts of the NHS are fully prepared, or if not have contingency plans in place, leaves them very little time to deal with problems that emerge. We look to the Executive to take strong and decisive action, including direct intervention where appropriate, to ensure that all NHS organisations and GPs are fully prepared (paragraph 51).

(ix) Many of the more sophisticated diagnostic and treatment services which the NHS use rely extensively on electronic equipment, and failure of those systems could have serious consequences for patients. We are therefore appalled that the Medical Devices Agency did not realise the potential impact of failures until late 1997. In our view, this delay, and the misleading advice they gave the NHS in 1996 can only have increased the risks to patients and the costs of remedial action (paragraph 52).

(x) We welcome the action the NHS has now taken to tackle medical equipment, their assurance that they were putting a premium on patient safety and the fact that the NHS has set aside £150 million to help replace equipment or parts affected by the year 2000 problem. But we are disturbed that the NHS Executive could not give us a categorical assurance on the safety of patients. We expect the NHS Executive to monitor the position on medical equipment closely, and to take every step possible to ensure the safety of patients (paragraph 53).

(xi) We note the NHS Executive confidence that the GP systems will be ready in time (paragraph 54).

(xii) We note NHS Executive's assurance that that expenditure on year 2000 work will not lead to any downgrading of patient care. However, we remain concerned about the possible impact on capital programmes of diverting money to year 2000 work; about the possible delay to other important projects; and about the added pressure on already stretched budgets. We expect the Executive to monitor closely the impact of the costs of tackling the year 2000 problem, and ensure that lack of resources do not result in the failure of systems and equipment that are critical to NHS services and patient care (paragraph 55).

PROGRESS MADE IN CENTRAL GOVERNMENT AND THE WIDER PUBLIC SECTOR

8. Although the responsibility for ensuring that government business continues without disruption in the year 2000 rests with each government department and agency, at the centre the Office of Public Service, through the Central Information Technology Unit and the Central Computer Telecommunications Agency have a monitoring, advisory and co-ordination role. Since 30 March 1998, this role has extended across the whole public sector.[3]

9. The Committee asked the Office of Public Service what accountability they had for ensuring that the problem was tackled successfully.   They told us that had to ensure that their own internal systems and those of their agencies were year 2000 compliant. In addition, they

[3] C&AG's report, (HC 724 of 1997–98), para 9

were accountable for ensuring that the Chancellor of the Duchy of Lancaster was properly advised, and had problems in other departments drawn to his attention, so that he could fulfil his responsibility for:

- monitoring the situation;

- drawing areas of concern to the attention of particular ministers;

- putting urgency behind the system; and

- disclosing the situation to public scrutiny.[4]

10. They added that originally these responsibilities covered central government, but in March 1998 had been extended to the wider public sector. Although the potential control of ministers collectively over the wider public sector was clearly less direct, they hoped to progressively increase the level of scrutiny and detail for at least the key areas.[5]

11. We asked what action the Office of Public Service could take if serious problems emerged through the monitoring process. They said that it would not be for them to instruct a department to take remedial action. But if the Chancellor of the Duchy was unhappy he would take it up with the relevant minister.[6]

12. The departmental progress reports published in November 1997 and March 1998 were of variable content and format and revealed slippage against completion targets.[7] In the light of these reports, we asked the Office of Public Service how confident they were that government business would be able to continue without disruption in the year 2000. They told us that these reports, and those in June 1998, showed slippage in the expected completion dates with some cases getting uncomfortably close to the year 2000, leaving no room for manoeuvre or error. Slippage on business critical systems was not very serious, and 85 per cent of the returns predicted completion for business critical systems by June 1999, which is about three months later than previously forecast. There had been a little more slippage on other systems, and 87 per cent of these were now predicted for completion in September 1999. They took the view, however, that this was not as bad as it seemed because bit by bit there was increased coverage of the less critical systems.[8]

13. We asked about the risks of running right up to the wire. The Office of Public Service pointed out that central government was now about 30 per cent of the way through the actual correction programme for business critical systems, and so were getting more of a handle on what was going on. They told us, however, that there were clearly some departments they were concerned about, particularly those declaring completion dates in the second half of 1999.[9]

14. The Committee asked the Office of Public Service whether they had undertaken a comprehensive assessment of the risks posed by a failure to achieve compliance in the wider public sector, and what assurance they could give us that the wider public sector could achieve compliance by year 2000. They told us they had not yet undertaken such an assessment. The June 1998 return was the first time they had attempted to put comprehensive information together for the wider public sector and more work was needed to fine-tune the analysis and ensure they had a comprehensive picture.[10]

15. They pointed out that ministers had drawn the year 2000 problem to the attention of all public bodies in May 1996 and that, although returns hitherto had been pretty sketchy, this did not necessarily imply that actual progress was unsatisfactory. They intended to increase the level of scrutiny, picking on certain key sectors where the risk was greatest and ensuring their returns

---

[4] Qs 7, 14
[5] Q7
[6] Qs 7, 14–15
[7] C&AG's report, (HC 724 of Session 1997–98), paras 1.8, 1.10, 1.15
[8] Qs 2, 59
[9] Q59
[10] Q69

were in similar detail to those being made for central government.[11]

16. The total cost of achieving year 2000 compliance in central government departments and agencies was estimated in November 1997 at £370 million. By March 1998 the estimate had risen by 6 per cent to £393 million.[12] The Office of Public Service told us that their latest estimate was £402 million spread over at least two financial years and probably three.[13]

17. We asked how confident the Office of Public Service were about the accuracy of this figure. They admitted that they would not be surprised if the estimate increased a little bit, but it was unlikely to do so at the same rate as in the past, if only because the proportion of work still undone was reducing all the time.[14]

18. The Prime Minister said on 30 March 1998 that estimates which put the total public sector cost at up to £3 billion were reasonable.[15] We asked the Office of Public Service how this figure had been arrived at. They told us that the figure was not a forecast, but one that had seemed reasonable to the Prime Minister. They added that the £402 million estimate was for central government including the armed forces. The figure for the NHS in England was up to about £320 million, though they did not have the figures for the NHS in Wales, Scotland or Northern Ireland. And for local government, the Local Government Association had put the cost at about £500 million. In total this added up to something short of £1½ billion. In addition, there were other areas of the wider public sector which they had mapped rather less well so far, such as London Transport, the Post Office, British Nuclear Fuels and the Civil Aviation Authority. Overall, they concluded that there was ground for thinking at £3 billion was probably in the right ball park.[16]

19. We asked the Office of Public Service how far the Government's IT programme would be delayed by the diversion of resources into combatting the millennium threat. They pointed out that of the £2 billion the Government spends each year on IT procurement and services, expenditure of £400 million over two or three financial years on the millennium threat was not hugely disproportionate. Tackling the threat had changed some priorities within programmes, accelerating replacements in some cases and postponing updates in others, but they had had no signs that diversion of resources had become a major worry to the departments.[17]

20. We asked the Treasury if it was their policy that year 2000 costs would be absorbed by Departments irrespective of any difficulties this might cause. They told us that the Government's current policy was that the costs should be met from within existing plans. However, as much of the activity would be replacement of hardware and software which may well have been a requirement in any event, not all of the £3 billion would be an additional call on resources. They were fairly confident that the Government would not allow a situation to arise where compliance would not be achieved because of financial constraints, and they assured us they would react sensibly to cost increases brought to their attention which could not be absorbed.[18]

21. Overall departments and agencies claim that they have the necessary skilled resources available in-house or from existing suppliers of contracted out services. However, there is a risk that as more detailed work is done, revealing the need for additional staff, sufficient staff will not be available or costs will rise as departments and agencies find they have to pay premium rates. Already the Ministry of Defence had signalled their concerns about emerging staff shortages.[19]

---

[11] Qs 7, 51, 69–74

[12] C&AG's report (HC 724 of Session 1997–98), paras 1.32, 1.36

[13] Qs 21, 30, 97

[14] Qs 21, 50, 98–101

[15] C&AG's report, (HC 724 of Session 1997–98) , paras 5 and 1.32

[16] Qs 26–29, and 85–86; and Appendix 1, p18

[17] Qs 90–91

[18] Qs 87, 147

[19] C&AG's report, (HC 724 of Session 1997–98), para 10

22. The Committee asked the Office of Public Service whether they were confident that sufficient skilled staff would be available. They told us that loss of skilled staff did not appear to be a problem, possibly because civil service employment tends to be a little less volatile than other areas. Many departments had outsourced the provision of IT services and they did not see serious signs of any failure of suppliers maintaining necessary staffing levels. Others, for example the Scottish Office, were seeking to retrain many people in these skills. So their assessment was that while staffing continued to be a matter of concern it had proved less of an issue than they had thought it might be.[20]

23. We asked whether the potential staffing difficulties reported by the Ministry of Defence posed any threat to our defence capability. The Office of Public Service said that the Ministry of Defence were concerned about skill supply shortage, but the general messages from them concerning strategic or operational risks were reassuring.[21] They were giving priority to those systems which were critical to maintaining the operational effectiveness of the Armed Forces, and were confident that all key operationally critical systems, including those relating to strategic defences would be rectified before problems were encountered.[22]

24. In view of the potential impacts of failures in computer systems and electronic equipment, effective contingency plans are essential. In his Report, the Comptroller and Auditor General noted that Departments and agencies needed to bring their business continuity plans up to date to deal with the impact of failure of their own systems and those of third parties.[23] We therefore asked Office of Public Service what action had been taken to ensure all bodies had adequate business continuity plans in place.   They told us it was a standing arrangement that right through government there were disaster plans to cover breakdowns, such as a failure of electricity. They assured us that all departments and agencies were engaged in bringing these plans up to scratch with specific reference to the year 2000 problem. These plans had to cope with problems in their own systems, with problems in the systems of third parties with whom they had electronic links, and with problems in non-IT suppliers including public utilities. About half the departments and agencies had year 2000 adjusted contingency plans in place though they varied in scope and detail.[24]

25. The Committee asked the Office of Public Service if it was possible to recover remedial costs from suppliers. The said that in their view it was wrong to imply that the Year 2000 issue was somebody's fault. A large part of what was being corrected was a failure to take account of the year 2000 problem in systems, some of which were installed a quarter of a century ago when people did not expect their systems or particular software programmes to last as long as that. [25]

26. They said that the Central Computer and Telecommunications Agency had issued guidance in September 1996 that provided for year 2000 compliance as a standard requirement on purchase of all new IT systems. And the general question of supplier liability was addressed in the six volume guidance the Central Computer and Telecommunications Agency had published. They had not issued a specific guidance letter on liability questions but it was a matter they were looking into.[26] They had undertaken some initial work on the question of legal liabilities, but the priority was to tackle the problem first and unless warranties had been given at that time, they thought it unlikely that damages could be claimed in most cases.[27] And it was for individual departments to tackle supplier liability, depending on the terms of individual contract or procurement.[28]

---

[20] Qs 4–6, 48

[21] Qs 102–110

[22] Supplementary Memorandum from the Office of Public Service, Evidence, Appendix 3, p19

[23] C&AG's report, (HC 724 of Session 1997–98, paras 6 and 1.29

[24] Q16

[25] Q31

[26] Qs 31–37, 80

[27] Qs 31–34

[28] Qs 75–76

Conclusions

27. Progress reports for central government already show some slippage and some Departments do not now expect to complete their work until the second half of 1999. As a result, we cannot be sure that government business will not be disrupted in the year 2000, and in some cases there is little room for manoeuvre if things go wrong. The Office of Public Service need to direct particular attention to those central government departments that do not expect to complete their work until the second half of 1999.

28. We are concerned that the estimated cost to central government bodies rose by 9 per cent between November 1997 and June 1998. However we note the view of the Office of Public Services that although costs may rise above the latest estimate of £402 million, they should not rise as rapidly as in the past.

29. We note the Office of Public Service's view that the £400 million required by central government can be found from within existing budgets, partly by rescheduling replacement programmes, without any further impact on services. And we are encouraged by the assurance from Treasury that if costs cannot be absorbed by departments they would react sensibly. We expect the Office of Public Services to draw the attention of Treasury to any areas where resource constraints put timely completion of the programme at risk.

30. We are disappointed that the first attempt to monitor progress across the wider public sector was in June 1998, some one and a half years after the programme began. This has prevented the Office of Public Service from undertaking a comprehensive risk assessment. In the absence of such an assessment, and in view of the patchy returns received so far, we are concerned about the readiness of the wider public sector to cope with the Year 2000 issue and about whether resources are being targeted on those business critical systems most at risk. We expect the Office of Public Service to complete a full risk assessment across the whole of the public sector by mid-1998, to identify bodies and key risk areas that should be targeted for action or intensive monitoring.

31. It is not possible to predict the full impact of the millennium threat within an organisation or through the supply chain. We are concerned, therefore, that only half of government departments and agencies have updated their business continuity plans to deal with the year 2000 and that those that exist vary in scope and detail. We look to the Office of Public Service to require all public bodies to have comprehensive, robust business continuity plans in place by January 1999.

32. We recognise that many of the systems and equipment that need to be replaced or modified were installed well before the scale of the Year 2000 issue became apparent. Nevertheless, we disappointed that the Office of Public Service has not given a stronger lead on the issue of supplier liability. We expect them to provide guidance and support to departments, agencies and the wider public sector to ensure that wherever possible suppliers that fail to meet their obligations meet the costs involved.

PROGRESS MADE IN THE NHS IN ENGLAND

33. The NHS relies heavily on IT systems and electronic equipment for many patient services. It is impossible to predict the seriousness of malfunctions, but in extreme circumstances failure or malfunction of equipment could put patients lives at risk. The Chief Executive of the NHS has described the year 2000 problem as the highest non-clinical priority in the NHS. There could be serious disruption to the NHS in the year 2000 unless urgent pre-emptive action is taken.[29]

34. Initially in May 1996 the NHS Executive set up a small project to assess what action needed to be taken, and alerted Trusts and Health Authorities to the problem and issued information packs. The Executive first wrote directly to Chief Executives of Health Authorities and NHS Trusts on the potential problems of the year 2000 date change in September 1996. They did not set a specific timescale for action, although they told Chief Executives that they

---

[29] C&AG's report, (HC 724 of Session 1997–98), paras 2.7–2.10

should know where they stood before the end of 1996. In October 1997, the NHS Executive instructed Chief Executives of NHS Trusts and Health Authorities to take personal responsibility for ensuring patient services were not compromised, and set timescales for action.[30]

35. The Committee asked the NHS Executive why they had set any deadlines in 1996. They told us that initially they had followed through with training events and information packs, and that they had monitored action in the early part of 1997. At that time, they found that the response had not been as good as they had wanted and this was one of the reasons why they had then set up the monitoring process against targets.[31]

36. The Comptroller and Auditor General reported that in October 1997, 10 per cent of NHS Trusts were not confident that their IT systems would be compliant by the end of 1999, and 15 per cent were not confident that their clinical equipment would continue functioning normally in the year 2000.[32]   We asked the NHS Executive how they would ensure all trusts were ready in time. They said they had now set very clear deadlines:

- a planning deadline of December 1998 when all critical systems should be fully ready and tested or, if they were not, there should be detailed plans to cope without those systems and equipment; and

- a final check deadline of September 1999 to ensure all parts of the NHS were either fully prepared or in some cases had proper contingency plans in place.[33]

37. The NHS Executive added that all the returns they had suggested that the two deadlines would be met across the NHS.   They were confident that everyone would meet their targets for fixing IT systems. However, they did not think everyone was confident of fixing their medical equipment, and this was one of the reasons why the NHS had set aside £150 million as a contingency sum.[34]

38. We asked if the deadline of September 1999 left them with enough time to sort out any problems, should difficulties emerge They were confident that good progress could be made during the period December 1998 to September 1999. They would be monitoring quarterly until the end of December 1999.   They would also be receiving regular reports from their district auditors and samples of the quarterly reports would be sent to an independent reference group. And although the responsibility for meeting the deadlines lay with each Trust Board and each Health Authority, regional offices would, and indeed had already intervened.[35]

39. We had previously examined the NHS Executive on the development of hospital information support systems.[36] We asked whether these systems would be millennium compliant, and what this would cost. The Executive assured us that all patient administration systems were being actively investigated by the individual trusts who ran them in conjunction with suppliers, and they expected all of them to be resolved in terms of year 2000 compliance problems by the dates they had set.[37] As regards the cost, they told us that of the nine sites involved, seven had maintenance agreements with suppliers which covered the costs. Of the two sites that did not have maintenance agreements, Nottingham City Hospital NHS Trust estimated the cost at £61,000 while the Birmingham Heartlands Hospital NHS Trust put the cost at £501,000.[38]

40. Many of the more sophisticated diagnostic and treatment services which the NHS use rely extensively on electronic equipment and failure of those systems could have serious consequences for patients.   Initially the Medical Devices Agency advised that while medical

---

[30] C&AG's report, (HC 724 of Session 1997–98), paras 2.16–2.22

[31] Qs 67–68

[32] C&AG's report, (HC 724 of Session 1997–98), para 13

[33] Qs 10, and 41–46

[34] Qs 132–138

[35] Qs 56–57, 95

[36] 7th Report of the Committee of Public Accounts, Session 1996–97, (HC 97)

[37] Qs 114–122

[38] Evidence, Appendix 2, p19

devices might show some year 2000 problems, these were unlikely to be serious and very unlikely to be life threatening. However, in October 1997 the NHS Executive instructed NHS organisations to draw up inventories of electronic equipment, prioritise equipment whose failures could have serious consequences, contact suppliers for advice, take corrective action if necessary and draw up contingency plans for equipment failure. The Medical Devices Agency issued a bulletin to all medical equipment manufacturers advising them to assess all their produces, identify any affected by the year 2000 problem and make this information available to users. They also emphasised the need to prioritise action, stating that resources did not exist to investigate every item of hardware and software in use, let alone to put right those affected by the problem.[39]

41. We asked the NHS Executive why the Medical Devices Agency was so late in recognising the potential threat. They agreed that it had taken some time for the whole question of embedded chips in electro-medical equipment to be given the same emphasis that had been given to IT systems, but that the Medical Devices Agency was now providing proper support to the NHS. They recognised that there are some pieces of equipment that are so critical and could not be tested in time. As a result, they had set aside £150 million as a contingency sum to enable replacement or renewal of parts.[40]

42. We asked the NHS Executive how they planned to ensure that no patients were exposed to risk from equipment or systems failure. They told us that the each NHS Trust was having to tackle the supply industry almost on an item by item basis. With thousands of different items of equipment in use, the Executive were following all available lines of enquiry. They were trying to obtain compliance information. They were being clear about testing procedures where these were relevant. They had agreed with the Medical Devices Agency that the initial check on each bit of equipment would be made by the appropriate person holding the equipment in the NHS, and by the manufacturer. They had established a clearing house, a database on which people could exchange information. And manufacturers had sometimes exchanged information with them. Where they thought there might be problems, they were ensuring that they had contingency plans in place.[41]

43. They admitted, however, that they could not guarantee that nobody would die as a direct result of year 2000 problems. But they assured us they had systematically assessed all the risks and would continue to deal with them up to December 1999, and that patients' safety was the premium on all they were doing.[42]

44. The Comptroller and Auditor General reported that the information available on the state of readiness in General Practice suggested GPs were likely to have difficulty in achieving year 2000 compliance. And almost one third of Health Authorities did not have confidence that GP systems would be year 2000 compliant in time.[43] We therefore asked the NHS Executive how they would make sure that every GP would be ready. They took the view that the problems in GP surgeries were a lot less serious than in other parts of the NHS. This was partly because manufacturers of GP systems had been very good in pushing compliance. In addition, the latest returns showed that more than 80 per cent of GPs were well aware of the problems in store. And they assured us that systems for cervical screening had been made year 2000 compliant in 1995.[44]

45. They also pointed out that all GP systems were going to have to be upgraded to accommodate the Government's objective of having the facility to pass information freely and electronically between hospitals and GP settings. So the combination of improved software and in some cases improved hardware meant that the problem in general practice could be properly resolved. They added though, that GPs had good paper back-up systems and these were an

---

[39] C&AG's report, (HC 724 of Session 1997–98) , paras 2.10, 2.18, and 2.24–2.26

[40] Qs 131, 139–143

[41] Qs 9, 92–93, 96

[42] Q96

[43] C&AG's report, (HC 724 of Session 1997–98), para 15

[44] Q11

important safety net.[45]

46. The NHS Executive have told NHS organisations that they should plan to meet the cost of their year 2000 compliance programme from within existing budgets. The Comptroller and Auditor General reported that inadequate resourcing increased the risk of failure, and was the single largest area of concern identified by respondents to the NAO survey about the difficulties they faced in tackling the year 2000 problem. The Comptroller and Auditor General also reported that the cost of tackling the year 2000 issue in the NHS was estimated at £230 million but could be much higher.[46]

47. We therefore asked the NHS Executive about the cost, and how they planned to ensure that the NHS had adequate resources to complete the programme. They told us that on the basis of information from each individual NHS Trust, GP and Health Authority at the end of March 1998, the cost would be £320 million in England. This was made up of £170 million to deal with all of the IT issues and £150 million as a contingency against problems with medical devices.[47]

48. This figure needed to be put in the context of annual NHS expenditure on IT of £200 million and nearly £1 billion on medical and surgical equipment. They thought that the purchase of certain bits of equipment or upgrades of software might be brought forward from the normal replacement cycle but that any displacement activity would be under the capital budget and would not impact on recurrent monies that pay for staff and NHS activity.[48]

49. The Committee sought further reassurance from the NHS Executive that every Trust would be able to fund its year 2000 programme without loss of service to its patients. The Executive assured us that the money would be allocated on a non-recurring basis, with £210 million of the £320 million being spent in 1998-99. They added that since May 1997, for the NHS in England, the Government had allocated an extra £1.7 billion and part of that was to deal with this pressure. Expenditure on year 2000 work would be insulated from the routine of Health Service spending and would not lead to any downgrading of patient care.[49]

Conclusions

50. In view of the potential impact of the year 2000 issue on NHS services and on patients, we are astonished that the NHS Executive got off to such a slow start in addressing the problem. The failure to set deadlines for action in September 1996 was a missed opportunity to ensure that all NHS bodies took the threat seriously. The action taken by the Executive subsequently means that they now have in place the elements of a well managed project.

51. We note that the NHS Executive are confident that all IT systems will be modified in time, and that medical equipment will either be modified or replaced where required. But we are concerned that the deadline of September 1999 for finally checking that all parts of the NHS are fully prepared, or if not have contingency plans in place, leaves them very little time to deal with problems that emerge. We look to the Executive to take strong and decisive action, including direct intervention where appropriate, to ensure that all NHS organisations and GPs are fully prepared.

52. Many of the more sophisticated diagnostic and treatment services which the NHS use rely extensively on electronic equipment, and failure of those systems could have serious consequences for patients. We are therefore appalled that the Medical Devices Agency did not realise the potential impact of failures until late 1997. In our view, this delay, and the misleading advice they gave the NHS in 1996 can only have increased the risks to patients and the costs of remedial action.

---

[45] Qs 19–20

[46] C&AG's report, (HC 724 of Session 1997–98), paras 2.54–2.56

[47] Qs 12, 24, 83–84

[48] Q54

[49] Qs 12, 130

53. We welcome the action the NHS has now taken to tackle medical equipment, their assurance that they were putting a premium on patient safety and the fact that the NHS has set aside £150 million to help replace equipment or parts affected by the year 2000 problem. But we are disturbed that the NHS Executive could not give us a categorical assurance on the safety of patients. We expect the NHS Executive to monitor the position on medical equipment closely, and to take every step possible to ensure the safety of patients.

54. We note the NHS Executive confidence that the GP systems will be ready in time.

55. We note NHS Executive's assurance that expenditure on year 2000 work will not lead to any downgrading of patient care. However, we remain concerned about the possible impact on capital programmes of diverting money to year 2000 work; about the possible delay to other important projects; and about the added pressure on already stretched budgets. We expect the Executive to monitor closely the impact of the costs of tackling the year 2000 problem, and ensure that lack of resources do not result in the failure of systems and equipment that are critical to NHS services and patient care.

PROCEEDINGS OF THE COMMITTEE
RELATING TO THE REPORT

Session 1997–98

MONDAY 15 JUNE 1998

Members present:

Mr David Davis in the Chair

Mr Geoffrey Clifton-Brown   Mr Christopher Leslie
Ms Jane Griffiths   Mr Andrew Love
Mr Phil Hope   Mr Alan Williams

Mr Bob Le Marechal, CB, Deputy Comptroller and Auditor General, was further examined.

The Committee deliberated.

Mr Frank Martin, Second Treasury Officer of Accounts, was further examined.

The Comptroller and Auditor General's report on Managing the Millennium Threat II (HC 724) was considered.

Mr Robin Mountfield, CB, Permanent Secretary and Mr Mark Gladwyn, Deputy Director, Central IT Unit, the Cabinet Office (Office of Public Service); and Sir Alan Langlands, Chief Executive, and Mr Frank Burns, Head of Information Management and Technology, the National Health Service Executive, were examined (HC 816-i).

*   *   *   *   *

[Adjourned till Wednesday 17 June at half past Four o'clock.

*   *   *   *   *

Session 1997–98

WEDNESDAY 22 JULY 1998

Members present:

Mr David Davis, in the Chair

Mr Alan Campbell   Mr Andrew Love
Mr Geoffrey Clifton-Brown   Mr Richard Page
Ms Maria Eagle   Mr Alan Williams
Ms Jane Griffiths

Sir John Bourn, KCB, Comptroller and Auditor General, was further examined.

The Committee deliberated.

*   *   *   *   *

Draft Report (Managing the Millennium Threat), proposed by the Chairman, brought up and read.

Ordered, That the draft Report be read a second time, paragraph by paragraph.

Paragraphs 1 to 6 read and agreed to.

Paragraph 7 postponed.

Paragraphs 8 to 55 read and agreed to.

Postponed paragraph 7 read and agreed to.

Resolved, That the Report be the Sixty-sixth Report of the Committee to the House.

Ordered, That the Chairman do make the Report to the House.

Ordered, That the provisions of Standing Order No. 134 (Select Committees (Reports)) be applied to the Report.

* * * * *

[Adjourned till Monday 16 November at half past Four o'clock.

MINUTES OF EVIDENCE

TAKEN BEFORE THE COMMITTEE OF PUBLIC ACCOUNTS

MONDAY 15 JUNE 1998

Members present:

Mr David Davis, in the Chair

Mr Geoffrey Clifton-Brown	Mr Christopher Leslie
Ms Jane Griffiths	Mr Andrew Love
Mr Phil Hope	Mr Alan Williams

MR R N LE MARECHAL, CB, Deputy Comptroller and Auditor General, was further examined.

REPORT BY THE COMPTROLLER AND AUDITOR GENERAL
MANAGING THE MILLENNIUM THREAT II (HC 724)

Examination of witnesses

MR ROBIN MOUNTFIELD, CB, Permanent Secretary and MR MARK GLADWYN, Deputy Director, Central IT Unit, Cabinet Office (Office of Public Service), SIR ALAN LANGLANDS, Chief Executive and MR FRANK BURNS, Head of Information Management and Technology, National Health Service Executive, were examined.

MR FRANK MARTIN, Treasury Officer of Accounts, was further examined.

Chairman

1. Welcome again, Mr Mountfield and Sir Alan Langlands. Congratulations on your honour, Sir Alan.

(Sir Alan Langlands) Thank you.

2. Today we are looking at the Comptroller and Auditor General's second report on Managing the Millennium Threat and I propose to start with progress across central government with Mr Mountfield, if I may. I am going to start with paragraph 1.8 in the report, if that helps you. Given the variability of compliance and gaps in coverage recorded in that paragraph and the slippage against completion targets set for departments and agencies, how confident are you that government business will be able to continue without disruption in the year 2000?

(Mr Mountfield) I think in answering that question I have to be very careful to draw a reasonable balance between sensible confidence and undue complacency. I think it would be very unwise for anybody to give any guarantees that everything will be all right on the night but what I think is important is that we analyse the situation systematically as far as we can and make sure everybody is doing their bit and monitor that regularly. The reports that the Chancellor of the Duchy announced a week ago do show some slippage in the expected completion dates. The slippage is not, so far as business critical systems are concerned, very serious, it is about a quarter on average and the position remains that 85 per cent of the returns predict completion for business critical systems by June 1999, which is about a quarter later than predicted previously. The slippage for all other systems is a little more than that—87 per cent of all systems are now

predicted for completion by September 1999. That is not necessarily quite what it seems to be because the coverage of the returns has been increasing bit by bit as the process of quarterly review has led managers to look more thoroughly at the areas to be investigated. So part of that is not so much slippage as increasing the coverage of the less critical systems. So far as cost is concerned—is that part of your question or do you want to come back to that?

3. Let us come back to that. I am sure a number of other members of the Committee will want to ask about that. Can I have in my mind some way of understanding this? Can you give me an example of what is considered a non-critical system?

(Mr Mountfield) I ought not to pretend the definition is very precise, it is left to the individual department or agency to classify its systems into critical or non-critical. Business critical is meant to imply those systems without which the agency or department could not continue normal business. There will clearly be a number of other systems where it is a matter of inconvenience, perhaps to staff, and it may cause delays but not things that frustrate the fundamental business of the agency or department. If you ask that of a front line, key department, like the DSS, which has a much greater impact on society than, let us say, a museum, the interpretation would reflect the judgment of the local manager rather than a systematic classification. It is no more than a guide, I think, to sensible prioritisation within each department and agency.

4. All right, we may come back to the examples. Paragraph 1.25 of the C&AG's report notes emerging

[**Chairman** *Cont*]

concerns in the Ministry of Defence about the availability of sufficiently skilled staff. How confident are you that staff in departments and agencies have the necessary skills to complete your plans?

(Mr Mountfield) As you know, this is a matter we have been concerned about for some time and the Chancellor of the Duchy has increased the intensity of questioning on that for that reason. Perhaps I can divide my answer into two parts. On the question of the loss of skills, the actual departure of people, the indication is that this is not yet emerging as a serious problem. About 14 per cent of returns report some loss but usually only one or two people, and where the numbers are slightly larger it is usually a large department with a big IT department where there is regularly some turnover and they are not reporting difficulties in replacing that loss. There is a separate question about whether the total quantity of skilled resource is adequate and about a third of the departments say this is an area of concern. The Ministry of Defence is one of the major ones and they say that what it is causing is some diversion of IT skills from other areas into year 2000 compliance. Overall, our assessment would be this continues to be a matter of concern but is proving so far to be less actual than we had previously thought.

5. The loss, as you describe it, may well go up exponentially as the price goes up?

(Mr Mountfield) Yes.

6. You mentioned in answer to my first question that the size of the apparent problem has been growing because people are looking more carefully. Would the demand for the required number of specialists not grow in the same way?

(Mr Mountfield) In principle, yes, but when I say the size is growing I think what I mean by that is that the peripheral, very often quite small systems, are being added to the scope of the survey. The indication of cost, if I may touch on that briefly, is that the cost is not seen as rising very substantially, and if that reflects the volume of work I do not think this is implying there is a huge increase in the volume of work that is predicted. On the problem of exponential difficulties in the skills area, obviously we are concerned about that because one hears reports in the private sector about very substantial salaries being paid for people with particular skills. In a way we have been asking ourselves why this has not yet emerged as a big problem, and one of the answers is that civil service employment tends to be a little less volatile than in other areas and people are looking beyond the year 2000 for continuity of employment rather than what they can make in the short term. That may be wishful thinking, we shall have to see, but the signs so far are not as bad as we thought.

7. Taking you on to paragraph 1.38—you have partly answered this but I think we ought to get it clearly on the record—that paragraph records the widening of your role to cover co-ordinating and monitoring across the wider public sector, a point your Minister made in the statement last week. What do you now see as your accountability for ensuring the problem is tackled successfully and what action can you take if you detect signs of failure or slippage?

(Mr Mountfield) First of all, if I may relate my own accountability to that of the Chancellor of the Duchy in relation to this: he is not, of course, in a ministerial sense directly responsible for every department across the sector, still less for the wider public sector. What he has been asked to undertake is responsibility for monitoring the situation, for drawing areas of concern to the attention both of the particular ministers and of ministers collectively as part of the process of making sure the priorities are right, that urgency is put behind the system, and also particularly making sure the emerging situation in some detail is disclosed to the public view in the belief that public scrutiny is one of the mechanisms by which managers will be brought face to face with their priorities where they are not, though I would not wish to imply by that that our general perception is that managers are not aware of the needs. The original responsibility of the Chancellor of the Duchy was for the central government area and, as you know, the Prime Minister, in a speech in March, said he was asking the Chancellor of the Duchy to extend that overview to the wider public sector. The potential control of ministers collectively over the wider public sector is clearly less direct than it is for central government—there are statutory bodies, locally elected bodies and so on—so it will be a matter for a departmental minister with sponsorship for a wider public sector area which may not be as great as it is for his or her own department. Nevertheless, what we hope to do progressively is increase the level of scrutiny and detail for at least the key areas of the wider public sector beyond, frankly, the rather patchy results we got in the first round.

8. I want to turn to Sir Alan now but I will come back to you, Mr Mountfield, at the very end, to take up this question of cost. I want to deal with the NHS first because there is a critical cost effect there which you might wish to comment on too. Welcome, Sir Alan, and congratulations again on your honour.

(Sir Alan Langlands) Thank you.

9. Turning now to paragraph 2.7, that paragraph records you have advised NHS trusts and health authorities that equipment failure could put patients' lives at risk, and some press reports put the number of risks up to 1,500 patients. How do you plan to ensure no patients are exposed to any risk from equipment or systems failure?

(Sir Alan Langlands) Possibly the first thing to say is that the press reports about numbers are pretty speculative. We are certainly doing all we can to prevent and minimise risk. We are having in relation to medical equipment to tackle from each NHS trust the supply industry almost on an item by item basis, because one has to be clear that every piece of equipment has been checked; it is not possible to batch-check, if you like. Certainly the Medical Devices Agency is helpful in the sense they are tackling the manufacturers on our behalf where we think there are specific problems, and they have been very good in disseminating information across the Health Service. The medical equipment industry is a global industry and they network with our colleagues in Scotland, USA and Canada. So we are in relation to medical equipment and systems following all the available

[Chairman *Cont*]

lines of enquiry that are open to us, trying to obtain compliance information, being clear about testing procedures where these are relevant, and where we think there might be particular problems ensuring we have contingencies in place to deal with these. So we are trying to avoid all of these risks and put patients' safety as the premium on all we are doing.

10. Thank you, Sir Alan. One of the points in the report was that 15 per cent, I think it was, of trusts were not confident that their medical equipment would work perfectly after the millennium. If you are confident the 1,500 figure being mooted by the press is wrong, please do not be bashful in saying so, this is a perfectly good public opportunity to do that. Can you be clear for us that that 15 per cent number will be eradicated?

(Sir Alan Langlands) The 15 per cent number we hope does not come into existence. We have set very clear deadlines for December 1998 and September 1999, and by December 1998 we want all critical systems to be fully ready and tested or, if they are not, for detailed plans to be made to cope without those systems and those bits of equipment. That is, if you like, a planning deadline. Then by 30th September 1999 we have a final check to ensure all parts of the NHS are either fully prepared or in some cases, in a sort of belt and braces way, to make sure proper contingency plans are in place. The 1,500 figure, I think, is attributed to someone, an expert, who also claims in a recent article that the NHS has the best organised millennium action project of any health service in the world. I do not know, and have no way of judging, whether or not that is true, but certainly there is rigour in how we are planning this and in how we intend to follow it through over the next 18 months.

11. Paragraphs 2.42 and 2.44 deal with the state of readiness, if that is the right word, in general practice. GPs do not seem to be taking this problem seriously enough, how will you make sure that every GP will be ready in time?

(Sir Alan Langlands) The first thing to be clear about is that the systems and problems in GP surgeries are a lot less serious than they are in other parts of the Health Service. Using the sort of coding in here, they are more like small businesses than large ones. I think it is also true to say that the manufacturers of GP systems have been very good in pushing compliance. Our latest returns, rather contradicting or improving on the figures you have seen here, show that more than 80 per cent of GPs are well aware of the problems that are in store. This is one area where the systems have already been tested. When I was here last time we were talking about cervical screening, which the Committee will remember is organised on a three or five year cycle, and these systems were made pre-2000 compliant in 1995 and there have been improvements in the prescription systems for GPs as well. So I am confident. Perhaps the single most important issue in this area, because there is a great variety of systems around GP surgeries, is that all GP systems are going to have to be upgraded to accommodate the Government's objective of having the facility to pass information freely and electronically between hospitals and GP settings. So the combination of improved software, which is in hand, and in some cases improved hardware, I think means that the GP problem can be properly resolved. Of course, there is in GP surgeries the fall-back of very well developed paper systems which have actually served the Service well for 50 years and still exist in 95 per cent of places.

12. You beat me to the punch on the question of the smear testing programme. How do you plan to ensure the NHS has adequate staff and financial resources to complete the programme and manage any slippage, given the concerns expressed in paragraphs 2.27 and 2.39?

(Sir Alan Langlands) When we were bidding for resources for the current year, and most of the expenditure will fall in the current year, this pressure was taken into account. Since May 1997 for the NHS in England the Government have allocated an extra £1.7 billion and part of that was to deal with this pressure. The information we had from each individual trust and GP and health authority at the end of March aggregates to a sum of £320 million required to deal with this problem; the lion's share this year and the balance next year. These are large sums but they are from a very substantial budget, the medical equipment budget and computing budget in the NHS, and people now, I think, after some initial concerns, are getting down to the task of making the necessary improvements from the available resources.

13. One of the problems of partially defined technical systems is that they almost invariably end up costing more than you think, and this is something we see in front of this Committee all the time. I have forgotten which paragraph it is but the report refers to the fact that your estimate of cost is at the low end of what equipment organisations might assess, are you not worried this is going to run away in the course of the next few years?

(Sir Alan Langlands) We cover a huge variety of organisations, from the single-handed GP to the major teaching hospital, so it is difficult to generalise. We reckon the cost for the bigger hospitals, the acute trusts, will be of the order of about £950,000, which is a lot of money. The benchmarks that run through the report, based on Cap Gemini's analysis, I think we have to be very wary of because we are, in the Health Service, a very people-intensive industry and, as the Committee know from other hearings, we are not particularly well-developed in terms of IT and information management systems, so these comparisons are at risk of being spurious. I checked the other day, for example, and found that one of BP's largest and most complex refineries employs 47 people. We are an organisation that spends 85 per cent sometimes of our money on people, and certainly between 70 and 85 per cent in most places, so I think the comparisons might be rather suspect. The other point I would make is that the total I have suggested, the £320 million, is not a Department of Health planning total, it is the aggregate of submissions made by every health authority, every trust and every GP in the country.

Chairman: I have overrun my time so I will come back on the matter of cost at the end.

Jane Griffiths

14.   This is for Mr Mountfield. I speak as someone who is a little sceptical about the existence of a serious millennium threat anywhere, but leaving that aside, Mr Mountfield, what is your accountability? If you observe, or if it is brought to your attention, that there is failure or slippage, which it looks from this report as though there could well be, though that could be anticipated, what is your accountability as regards to that? What can you do to prevent or remedy it?

(Mr Mountfield)   Could I distinguish two areas in my answer? First of all, I am answerable as accounting officer for the OPS for our own internal systems in the OPS and its agencies. That, of course, is relatively small but it is important we should make sure they are properly handled. Secondly, for the wider position, because the Central IT Unit and the Central Computer and Telecommunications Agency are part of the Department and they are advising ministers, particularly the Chancellor of the Duchy on his quarterly return process, my accountability is to make sure he is properly advised, that problems are drawn to his attention in other departments, so that he can pick them up either in a general way or by specifically raising it with the responsible minister. Following the June statement last week, the Chancellor of the Duchy expects to write to every single minister in charge of a department raising some particular points, in other words not a general round robin letter but raising particular points on the returns for the agencies or wider public sector organisations that that minister is responsible for. Over the period since we started the quarterly return process in November last year, there have been well over 100 individual interactions between CITU or CCTA and individual departments about specific problems the returns have raised. So we are engaged in quite a detailed process of questioning where there are uncertainties which have emerged from the returns, areas where we think there is at least a question to be asked. It is very much a probing and monitoring exercise in order to direct the attention of local managers to their own responsibilities.

15.   That outlines your accountability as regards the monitoring process, but what action can you have taken, or seek to have taken, if a serious problem emerges as part of that monitoring process?

(Mr Mountfield)   Of course, if a problem emerged in Department X or Agency Y, it would not be for us to instruct that department to do it, that is not the way the ministerial system works. It would rather be for the Chancellor of the Duchy to raise questions, and if he were unhappy about the extent to which notice was being taken of the questions it would be raised by the Chancellor of the Duchy with the relevant minister.

16.   On continuity planning, the C&AG report is a little worrying in paragraphs 1.29 and 1.30. The returns did not really indicate that most bodies thought they had adequate plans to begin with, and there was even a small proportion who thought that such plans were not necessary at all. Can you comment on that?

(Mr Mountfield)   It is again to some extent a problem of definition and what one means by "a continuity plan". So far as business critical IT systems

right through Government are concerned, it is a standing arrangement, as you would expect, that there are disaster plans for a break-down, for example if electricity goes down or something like that. All departments and agencies are therefore now engaged in bringing those plans up to scratch with specific reference to the year 2000 problem. The range of issues that those have to cope with are in three areas. First of all, problems that go wrong within the system. For example, it may be that for all the best endeavours a problem has not been tracked in a particular system and it goes down as a result of that. The second area is if suppliers, particularly IT interfaces with outside bodies, go down not because the department's own system goes down but the one they relate to goes down. The third is non-IT supplies, for example, electricity, gas, utilities generally or something of that kind goes down, or other key suppliers are in default. Each of those needs some sort of response and I think the position at the moment is that about half the departments and agencies now have year 2000-adjusted continuity plans. All of them have a target date for completion—if they have not got it already they all have a target date for completion—but I think it ought to be said they vary in scope and detail. To some extent that is understandable because if you are a very small agency with very little business critical activity, it may not matter very much if relatively minor bits of kit go down, for others clearly it is very important indeed there are fall-back arrangements, particularly where health and safety is concerned, payment of staff or payment of members of the public through the benefit system are concerned. So there are quite a number of layers of seriousness in this and that has to be taken account of in the continuity planning system. There is one further layer which I ought to refer to, which is the general civil emergencies machinery. As you will know, there is a standing civil emergencies machine in Government run by the Home Office. That continues in operation clearly and is being tuned up to address particularly problems which arise from year 2000. The Emergency Planning College which gives training to people right through the public services on these matters is doing some courses on year 2000 planning. That is a separate end of the thing and at the most general end of the contingency planning.

17.   A question to Sir Alan—in paragraph 2.4 of the Report in part 2, it indicates that parts of the NHS risk not only not being ready and equipped with compliant systems by the millennium, but, more worryingly to me, not able to manage the consequences of non-compliance. It seems to me that nobody quite knows what the consequences of not having compliant systems might be and it is, therefore, important to be prepared for all possible eventualities, but this Report at this late stage in the middle of 1998 indicates that there are parts of the NHS which do not believe, by their best understanding, that they are able to manage the consequences. What should be done to address that and what can be done?

(Sir Alan Langlands)   Well, I think quite a lot has been done because although the Report was only published a short time ago, the snapshot in the Report

[Jane Griffiths *Cont]*

was taken in October 1997 and I think things have improved since then. I think people are much clearer about what is required and, as I answered the Chairman's question about the two critical dates of December 1998 and September 1999, I do have confidence that people are now fixed on the notion that all critical systems must be ready and tested or that detailed plans have to be made to cope with the possibility of failure. I think that is now clear throughout the Health Service and people are working consistently on that basis, and certainly our own monitoring is showing figures that exceed and provide a more positive picture than the Report provided when it did its review in 1997.

18. Sir Alan, a considerable amount of resources have been and are being devoted to ensuring compliance for the millennium and there is worldwide quite an industry of consultants who are operating in this field and selling their skills to organisations which may not be able to do it in-house. How is it possible to ensure that this considerable amount of public money which is devoted to this effort is used in the right way? Consultants may well be very expensive and the threat may well be not as great as one believes, but that has to be ensured before any money is spent at all, so how can it be ensured that the resources are directed where they should be?

(Sir Alan Langlands) Well, the first point to make is that there is an established group of people in the Health Service who have expertise in these sort of areas and I do not just mean the IT specialists, but I mean clinicians who use these systems and their technical support staff. They will tend, on issues like this and indeed the routine issues, to have good and effective working relationships with manufacturers and suppliers and often these will be covered contractually. Where people do use consultants in support, my belief is that the vast majority, if not all, of health bodies will have at least a critical mass of people who can act as the informed clients, if you like, who would set the specification for any work being carried out externally very clearly and would be consistently checking that that work, which would have been subject to competition, was properly followed through, so all the usual checks and balances are in place on this issue, as they would be on any contractual issue.

19. Some of my colleagues might want to come back on that, but just finally, do you think, Sir Alan, in your personal opinion, that you might have cause to be grateful in the future to the old-fashioned GP who keeps all his or her records on a card index in a shoe box?

(Sir Alan Langlands) Well, I do not know. I said earlier that GP systems are less critical in terms of some major hospital systems, but they certainly are important in terms of the convenience factor. It is the case that we do have good paper back-up and indeed even in the small percentage of GPs who run electronic systems, we are bound to have proper back-up systems and back-up tapes for all of these, so we do have that fall-back position in general practice. Our aim, however, is to move on from the paper-based position in general practice and we have been set a target by our own ministers of achieving that change for most

practices by the end of the year 2000, so this is an important discipline along that track, but we will have the back-up on the 1st January 2000.

20. So that means no in answer to my question?

(Sir Alan Langlands) I think I am saying yes, that the paper back-up could be an important safety net in general practice.

Mr Leslie

21. Mr Mountfield, I would just like to pin down this whole business of the cost of this whole debacle really, the whole millennium threat. I know that some people see it as a problem, whereas others do not, but we do not really know and it is difficult to pin down before the facts, but can you give us a definitive outline of what is your current best guess estimate for the total of all government departments and then possibly the two big ones which I think are the Ministry of Defence, which the Report says will take a significant slice, and the National Health Service?

(Mr Mountfield) Well, first of all, so far as central government is concerned, as you know, we have been monitoring this for three successive quarters and the number has risen, which is not, I think, surprising, but not perhaps as much as people would think. Now, it would be foolish, I think, to be confident that it will not continue to rise, but equally I think we can now begin to take a little comfort from the fact that these are not shot-in-the-dark estimates, but the aggregation of detailed estimates by professionals who are already part-way through the task, so I think one is beginning to firm up a little bit and one can, I think, have a little more confidence, not least, if I can give one example, in that some departments have clearly had to increase their estimates, and some of them by proportionately quite large amounts, though they are not large in absolute sums, because they have taken in an extra chunk of risk that they had not accounted for, perhaps the embedded systems risk. Others, on the contrary, have reduced costs which implies that those who are actually implementing the changes are finding that the problem is less big than they thought. You mentioned the Ministry of Defence; they have an overall figure of £200 million which is included within the £402 million for central government. That includes broadly the Civil Service activities, but also the Armed Services.

22. So there is £402 million for all of them and the Ministry of Defence is about £200 million?

(Mr Mountfield) £200 million, yes.

23. What about the National Health Service?

(Mr Mountfield) Well, Sir Alan, I think, is much more able to answer.

24. Well, Sir Alan, can I just ask you that specific point, the total global NHS cost?

(Sir Alan Langlands) £320 million.

25. So I need somehow to reconcile these figures because the total government figure cannot be then £402 million.

(Mr Mountfield) The NHS is not included in the central government figure because that is treated as a separate category.

[Mr Leslie *Cont]*

26.   So it is £402 million plus £320 million?

(Mr Mountfield)   Indeed, but of course there are other areas of the wider public sector which I think we have mapped rather less well so far and that is an area that I think we will want to——

27.   So we do not know about local government, for example?

(Mr Mountfield)   We know something. The local government area has been estimated by the Local Government Association, on the basis of the Audit Commission's earlier work, at about £500 million, so that gives you quite a large part of the wider public sector, but there is still, for example, the area of non-departmental public bodies, the TECs, the——

28.   Well, there are all sorts of other quangos.

(Mr Mountfield)   There are things like London Transport, the BBC, the Post Office, British Nuclear Fuels, the Civil Aviation Authority and so on. The bits for which we have a number so far, which is central government, including the Armed Services, the NHS and local government, albeit rather generalised numbers for some of those, add up to something short of £1½ billion. I think the £3 billion for the wider public sector—the Prime Minister said in his speech in March that he was not explicitly backing that number, but he said it seemed a reasonable order of magnitude. I think there is some ground for thinking that is probably the right ball park.

29.   Right.

(Mr Mountfield)   If I could illustrate that by saying that if our figure of £400 million is about right for the roughly 700,000 people in central government and the armed services together, that is about 13 or 14 per cent public sector employment.

30.   That is an absolutely astronomical amount of money. Can you in any way tell me how we are going to recover some of this cash because what seems very strange to me in all of this is we are talking about spending all of this taxpayer's money to rectify a problem which is essentially something caused not by the public sector but by the people who sold us this duff and ineffective information technology equipment in the first place. How are we going to recover this?

(Mr Mountfield)   First of all, if I could answer on the question of scale. £400 million sounds an awful lot of money but that is spread over at least two financial years, probably three, with running costs for central government and the operational costs of the armed services running at about £30 billion a year, it is a very small increment.

31.   Sure. Let us get on to the recovery question. I am very anxious that we do not just spend this taxpayer's money when there might be a way of getting it back from the people responsible for getting us into this mess in the first place.

(Mr Mountfield)   I think it would be wrong to imply that this is in some sense somebody's fault. A large part of what is being corrected is failure to take account of the year 2000 problem in systems, some of which were installed a quarter of a century ago when people did not expect their systems or particular software programmes would last as long as that.

32.   A lot of it is still quite recent equipment.

(Mr Mountfield)   Some of it is quite recent. Of course in terms of how much can be recovered, the liability and so on, it will depend very much on what warranties were given at the time.

33.   Is anybody looking at that, seeing whether we can perhaps sue some of these companies for all the costs we are likely to incur in the public sector?

(Mr Mountfield)   There has been some initial work but the priority must be, I think, first of all, to crack the problem itself so far as we can and make sure that things are put right.

34.   Sure.

(Mr Mountfield)   We are pretty clear that unless warranties were given at the time, it is pretty unlikely that we will be able to claim damages in most cases now but it will depend on what assurances were given and the circumstances of individual purchases.

35.   If you or I bought a car and the engine was going to implode, and we knew this, in the year 2000, we would take it back to the garage that sold it to us and ask them to sort it out. What I am concerned about is why are we not doing the same sort of thing for a lot of the equipment that we do know is still within its guarantee or recently bought? For example, can you tell me are we absolutely sure that we are not still buying equipment that is not year 2000 compliant?

(Mr Mountfield)   First of all, so far as the big purchases are concerned, anything that has been purchased for some time past has been warranted year 2000 compliant, that has been in the standard terms and conditions for big procurement for some time. For smaller parts of IT kit all departments are now following the guidance which was issued by the Central Computer and Telecommunications Agency in September 1996 which provides for year 2000 compliance as a standard requirement. Of course some of the problem is in embedded systems which are not IT systems as such which are bought for other purposes and I think judgments have to be made in particular cases about how far we can write that in. One does not write year 2000 compliance into paper-clip purchasing, for example.

36.   Just out of interest, when was the whole problem of year 2000 compliance identified in the public arena? When did we know about it and when could we have expected IT companies to have reasonably made sure that their equipment was compliant?

(Mr Mountfield)   I think how far one can reasonably expect that is a big question. Sir Alan was mentioning, for example, the cervical screening, which was identified in 1995. CCTA began their concern about year 2000 compliance in November 1995 and things began to move quite seriously during the course of 1996.

37.   Have we been able to tie in in any way which particular information technology companies have the greatest compliance difficulties? Do we have any indication whether it is lap top or table top PCs we are talking about here or is it the actual software products?

[Mr Leslie *Cont]*

(Mr Mountfield) I am not aware of any general conclusions of that kind. I think it is probably widely spread through both software and hardware, depending on how far back it goes. The general expectation is that quite a lot of IT kit these days does not last all that long because it is obsolescent quite quickly and, therefore, renewal patterns have been assumed in purchasing plans for quite a long time. That is part of the solution to the problem and I know the renewal programmes are very substantial in the normal course for ordinary business reasons and that wraps up part of the year 2000 problem as we go along.

38. I remember last week during the statement one Member referred to Windows 95, which is probably what most of us are familiar with, not necessarily being compliant. Do you know about that particular example?

(Mr Mountfield) I wonder if I could ask Mr Gladwyn, who is the Deputy Director of the Central IT Unit, to answer that one.

(Mr Gladwyn) Yes. Mr Derek Wyatt asked that question. The specific Microsoft position on Windows 95 is that it is compliant with minor issues. Minor issues relate to the placing of certain patches, which are available for free download on the Internet, which may be necessary in certain circumstances. Punctiliously Mr Wyatt is correct, the programme is not 100 per cent compliant but it can be made compliant to match whatever needs.

39. Where I am going here is obviously Windows 95 was the new period we were looking at when the whole thing was available. We know Bill Gates, Microsoft, multi-billion pound profit making organisation, should they not be taking some sort of responsibility for what is going on in the public sector? Are we not looking to them to help us out given that a lot of the problem that there is might well be their doing?

(Mr Mountfield) In terms of actual corrective action I have no doubt they are. The example that Mr Gladwyn has just given of fixing particular problems in Windows 95 is one way in which the manufacturers and suppliers are helping. The question of liability is a very big question which of course is not just a public sector one, it applies right through the economy. That is why I am advised it is quite a complex one and it is not all that easy, unless there are clear contractual commitments in terms of sale, to attach liability to suppliers.

40. This was said also in the case in America when we were looking at tobacco and whether tobacco was seen as necessarily causing cancer and of course we now know a lot of liability has been accepted by some of these people even though they did not given written guarantees or warranties, so surely I think there may be some degree of liability which will need to be chased up.

(Mr Mountfield) I understand that.

41. I hope that will be followed through. I just want to turn then to Sir Alan about the National Health Service and the time you have left in which to meet your compliance deadline of 31 December 1998. There are only 110 working days left until that time from today. Is that really a realistic deadline?

(Sir Alan Langlands) I am not sure about your arithmetic.

42. Five days a week.

(Sir Alan Langlands) 110 working days until the 31 December 1999 deadline?

43. 1998.

(Sir Alan Langlands) Yes.

44. That is not very many.

(Sir Alan Langlands) It is not very many.

45. Few weeks off sick.

(Sir Alan Langlands) As we said earlier, we have been working on very specific aspects of this problem since 1995. We have been working more generally since 1996. We are making progress. We have made a lot of progress I think between October 1997 and March 1998 but there is no doubt in my mind just from visiting the Health Service regularly that people are seized with the idea of getting on with this and getting it right. They now understand the resource position which perhaps was not as clear in September and October 1997 as it is now.

46. The urgency is also something we need to understand. Literally we are talking days before we need to have that compliance deadline met.

(Sir Alan Langlands) The urgency is very clear. I did use the phrase in answering the Chairman that the 31 December 1998 was a planning deadline and was quite precise about what needed to be done then. There is then a final check later in the year, in September.

47. Finally then—I have been given a yellow card—tell me whether it is possible to do a test run of any sort in different aspects of the National Health Service, maybe looking at focussing on a random sample of GP surgeries or different aspects within the NHS? Is it possible to isolate a small sample, turn the clock forward a little bit to see what happens, to try and get to grips with this? I am not quite so sure but is it possible to have a test run?

(Sir Alan Langlands) It is possible to test in some instances and I think there is the example in the Report from King's College Hospital about how they are carrying out the testing process, but the more complex and the more we are concerned with patient safety, the more I think we have to be careful about testing and ensuring that the manufacturers are involved in that process and that there is a system whereby, in particular, the complex tests, we will possibly witness the testing process, but one has to be cautious. There are some bits of testing that may prove irreversible, so it is a very technical area and one in which we are treading very carefully with the advice of the Medical Devices Agency and others.

Mr Love

48. Good afternoon, Mr Mountfield. Can I take you back to the issue of staffing that you touched on earlier with the Chairman? Really I want to ask you the question on staffing in relation to the issue of expertise in this particular area, but, most particularly,

[**Mr Love** *Cont*]

how the staffing issue interacts with the timescale that you are now operating to because you did say that of course civil servants tend to be in less volatile employment and no one wants to leave up to the year 2000 and then find themselves out of a job, but, as I understand it from most other private sector employers, it is not the case of retaining their existing staff, but indeed increasing their numbers of staff which I presume is a function of the timescale they are operating to. To what extent is the public sector under a similar pressure of not just needing to retain their staff, but needing to increase the number of staff they have in order to live up to that 2000 timescale?

(*Mr Mountfield*) I am sure that there is some problem of this kind and that is why we are concerned about it. On the other hand, I think one has to remember two or three things and, first of all, that tackling the year 2000 problem tends to be part of a programme of continual updating and modernisation of software systems and hardware systems, replacements and so on, and it is to some extent a question of adjusting priorities within that so that some tasks might get left until next year within the given resource. Secondly, although I referred to the Civil Service, of course a lot of departments have outsourced the provision of IT services and there are contractual obligations on the supplier to do the work and at the moment we do not see serious signs of any failure by outsourced suppliers to maintain the necessary staff levels. In some cases, there are one or two departments that have expressed concern about this. For example, the Lord Chancellor's Department is increasing the extent of its contracting out of these activities as a response to it. Another, again as an example, the Scottish Office, is seeking to retrain more people in these skills which of course is also being done for the economy as a whole. So there are a number of possible avenues to explore and I do not think I would want to imply that we are absolutely confident that this is not going to be a difficulty, but it does not, as I said before, seem to be so far quite as bad as we thought it was going to be.

49. I am going to come on to the issue of costs as I think the contracting out will impact on that, but before I do, there is some indication that the private sector, or at least parts of the private sector may have woken up to this problem earlier than the public sector did and if they are now at the stage where they are now rushing around trying to find the expertise to ensure that they comply by the year 2000, do you not have some concerns that this may be a crunch question for you in the next six months?

(*Mr Mountfield*) Yes, and I would certainly not want to assert that we have not got a problem. All I can say at the moment is that it is proving immediately less obvious on the ground than we thought it would be.

50. Can I take you on to the issue of costs because you did say that the central government costs are, I think it was, £402 million which is slightly higher than the figure given in the Report, so with the amount of outsourcing that you have already indicated is going on, how confident are you that that figure for central government, and I will come on to other parts later,

but how confident are you that that figure is relatively close to the real estimate of what it will be?

(*Mr Mountfield*) I would be surprised if on general grounds that number did not creep up a little bit because these things, as the Chairman has said, do tend to, but I draw a little bit of reassurance from how slow that increase is proving to be so far as the professionals get further into the detail, and I do stress that these are not figures drawn from the air in aggregate, but they are drawn from a collection of very detailed estimates by individual departments.

51. Can I take you on to the non-departmental public bodies? I get the impression both from the Report and the answers which were given earlier that to some extent all the other parts of the wider public sector, excluding local government and others, seem to be falling to some extent through a net. Your Department has direct responsibility for central government, but that wider public sector which we have only recently come to talk about does seem to be being missed out, so what confidence can you give us that whoever it is who is looking after that wider public sector has got a handle on it?

(*Mr Mountfield*) Perhaps I could distinguish two things. First of all, the actual level of preparation by bodies in the wider public sector, whether they are NDPBs or whatever: the existence of the year 2000 problem has been drawn to their attention by ministers since Mr Heseltine drew it to the attention of his colleagues in, from recollection, May 1996 and that was passed on to the managers of all the bodies concerned. But obviously the managers are very well aware of it as a problem, so the fact that our returns hitherto have been pretty sketchy, I do not think necessarily implies that the actual progress is unsatisfactory. So far as the returns are concerned, as you know, the Prime Minister asked the Chancellor of the Duchy to extend his survey to the wider public sector, including NDPBs, in March and the June return is the first result. The material that was put out on the Internet and in the Library of the House gives a fair amount of detail by specific bodies. I am sure you will have seen it. It goes down to the level of individual NDPBs, some of them very small and some of them much more important. What is clear, I think, is that there is not yet the degree of consistency of treatment in the returns that we would like to work towards. On the other hand, the wider public sector is a very large collection of bodies and ministers, I think, are likely through their discussions so far to want to pick on certain key sectors where the risk is greatest and concentrate on making sure that their returns are in similar detail, whether precisely the same or broadly analogous, to the returns which are being made for central government and that is where I would expect the iteration of returns to increase in the wider public sector.

52. Can I just press you on that because earlier on you said that the Secretary of State was attempting to find out the emerging situation so that that could be subject to public scrutiny and, therefore, getting in that information, and what I want to know is that there is talk in the Report about carrying out periodic surveys and making sure that you get standardised information,

[**Mr Love** *Cont*]

but is all of that work going on and are you confident that you will be getting in the information necessary to submit it to the public scrutiny that is necessary in order to achieve compliance by the year 2000?

(Mr Mountfield) I think we are reasonably satisfied with the shape of our questionnaire for central government bodies. Our objective is to apply that where it is appropriate, and it may not be in all cases, to wider public sector bodies if they are key sectors. Now, Sir Alan is better able to answer than I for the arrangements of the NHS, but that is an example where it may be that that particular format is not appropriate, but broadly similar information is now being prepared at the level of the individual authority and unit and the Chancellor of the Duchy and his colleagues are putting increasing emphasis on public scrutiny and putting material into the public domain whether on the Internet or by some similar means.

53. Can I come on to Sir Alan and congratulate you on the weekend announcement. Can I ask you about the cost within the NHS? You mentioned £320 million and what I am interested in is the impact that that cost will have within the wider NHS.

The Committee was suspended between 5.29 pm and 5.35 pm for a division in the House.

Mr Love: If I can carry the football analogy on, I hope a little extra time will be added.

Chairman: Injury time.

Mr Love

54. Sir Alan, can I come back to the question of the costs of compliance in the Health Service and in particular the impact that is likely to have on all the other services. Can you reassure us that this will not be having a negative impact on other capital expenditure or other aspects within the service?

(Sir Alan Langlands) Well, we spend a lot on capital and a lot on equipment replacement every year: 200 million on IT and 100 million on other things. In addition to that, under the whole medical surgical equipment heading we spend nearly a billion a year. So again we need to put that sum into perspective. I think it may be that the purchase of certain bits of equipment or certain upgrades of software, or whatever the issue may be, are brought forward from one year to another, from the normal replacement cycle. So to that extent you could argue that we might displace other things. Certainly any displacement activity will be under the capital budget in relation to non-recurrent monies and not in relation to recurrent monies that essentially pay for staff and Health Service activity.

55. You do not have any fears? There is always a great deal of talk about the cost of medical advance within the NHS, you have no fear that the capital budget will be diverted in a way that is going to impact on the time available through the Health Service?

(Sir Alan Langlands) We are in a stronger financial position this year than we have been for some time. We hope that will continue when we hear the results of the Comprehensive Spending Review.

56. So do we all. Can I move on to the deadline that you quoted in an earlier answer, December 1998

and September 1999. I just wondered if you felt in particular that September 1999 left you enough time should difficulties emerge during that period between December 1998 and September 1999? In effect, if there are problems that do arise you are going to leave yourself with very little time to sort them out.

(Sir Alan Langlands) I quoted these two deadlines because, if you like, they are the landmark deadlines but of course there will be quarterly monitoring in between times. Every quarter from now until the end of December 1999 we will monitor through our own system which does follow broadly the pattern for the Government as a whole and is customised to suit the Health Service essentially. Secondly, we will be having regular reports from our district auditors through the Audit Commission. Thirdly, when we do have these regular quarterly reports of our own we are sending some of them out, samples out, to an independent reference group so there are checks built into the system between December 1998 and September 1999 that will ensure that essentially people are doing what they say they are going to do during that period. We have been very clear, perhaps given the structure of the Health Service uncharacteristically so, that this has got to be handled on a line management basis and that the regional offices of the NHS Executive will intervene when they think people are not keeping pace with the plans they have set out. I am confident good progress can be made through that period.

57. That brings me on naturally to the other question I want to finish on which is this issue of intervention. What arrangements have you put in at the central organisation to intervene? This would be unusual within the Health Service and I just wondered what arrangements you have made to intervene and how that will happen? Perhaps you could tell us in terms of trusts and health authorities?

(Sir Alan Langlands) It is becoming more usual but essentially we have identified a line management relationship. Clearly the responsibility lies with each trust board and each health authority but I am using, if you like, the relationship I have with these chief executives in health authorities and trusts who will be the responsible people and health authorities responsible also for general practice essentially to effect a line management relationship. The people who will intervene on my behalf are the regional directors, the eight regional directors around the country. Also we have a national steering group set up run by one of these regional directors with the powers of intervention and also we have our own central project team who can intervene, if you like, in a positive way by disseminating good practice and information across the piece. This has been run as a pretty centralised operation with a lot of accountability and a lot of leverage from the centre.

58. In relation to that, can I just finish on the issue of general practitioners. You mentioned earlier the different reasons why you felt that perhaps general practitioners were not as much of a problem and certainly I accept that in terms of the clinical issues. Of course general practitioners are the gateway to the Health Service for the vast majority of people who

[**Mr Love** *Cont*]

come into it and of course patient records are an extremely important part of that relationship. If anything was to happen across the country that was likely to interfere with that relationship it could have a very adverse non-clinical effect. I want some reassurance you are taking that issue seriously?

(Sir Alan Langlands) I do and I do not trivialise the problems and the issues of general practice. I think the awareness is much higher than it was in the original report. I think the major software suppliers have year 2000 compliance very much in hand in that area. We have our own accreditation systems running. For the reasons I outlined earlier, the general upgrading of systems that the Government wants to pursue in general practice, we will be over the next year or so uprating a great deal of the hardware. We do not take these problems lightly and we do have some leverage in that area because although general practitioners have independent contractor status the reimbursement of payment for GP systems has to be on the basis of accredited systems. We are using that as a means of ensuring good practice in that area.

Mr Hope

59. Can I turn to figure one of the report on page 14 that basically describes the target dates for completion of compliance. I just wondered—this is obviously to Mr Mountfield—whether you feel we are taking things right up to the wire here? It seems to me that you are looking at 14 returns showing that it is going to be April 1999 or later before we have completion of reports. Do you not think we are running the risk of taking it right up to the wire and therefore no room for manoeuvre, no room for error, in the final analysis on a significant chunk of Central Government delivery?

(Mr Mountfield) As I have said before, I do not want to imply any complacency about this. It is clear that some cases are getting uncomfortably close to the wire and the Chancellor of the Duchy said that in his statement. If I can just recall, what we have done in the latest return is to ask departments and agencies to classify the business critical systems from the less critical systems and from the embedded systems and the telecom systems. We have a four way split. Of the business critical systems, which is the most troublesome area clearly, we are now showing 85 per cent expecting to be complete by June 1999. As time goes by and we get further into the programme I think those figures begin to acquire rather more reliability and authority. We are, for example, we believe about 30 per cent of the way through the actual correction programme for the business critical systems. We are getting more of a handle on what is going on. There are clearly some departments which we are concerned about, some of the ones declaring completion dates in the second half of 1999. I am not sure that is necessarily quite what it seems to be. For example, the Ministry of Defence is showing in the return that went on the Internet or put in the Library of the House that for all their systems they are predicting December 1999 completion. That is because largely for security reasons, relating to some military systems, they have aggregated all their systems into one return. I

understand that actually they expect it to be 80 per cent complete through their business critical systems by mid 1999 and well on even with the other 20 per cent. I think one has to be able to interpret even returns that are broken down by system. Nevertheless, there are clearly some areas of concern and I think the object of the quarterly monitoring is to put continued pressure on managers to adjust their priorities and deal particularly with the most serious ones.

60. The Ministry of Defence are particularly highlighted in the Report. Have you received assurances or has anybody received assurances that there is no threat to our defence capability as a result of the failure to comply?

(Mr Mountfield) Not on those terms. The Ministry have included, as I say, a single return, but we have informal discussions with the people monitoring the overall programme which is of course huge with many, many thousands of individual systems right through the civilian department and the operational end of the Armed Services and I think we are confident that it is being taken at least as seriously there as anywhere else, but complete assurance on every single system I think is probably a step too far.

61. Would you think it reasonable to expect the Ministry of Defence to be able to give us the reassurance that there is no threat to our defence capability as a result of this issue?

(Mr Mountfield) I am quite clear that it is a very high priority for them to make sure that all their operational priorities are deliverable, in other words, that all their systems are operational when needed.

62. Yes, "will be", but is it fair for us to expect the Ministry of Defence to issue some clear statement perhaps in private in some way because of issues of security and to expect that by a date well before December 1999 our defence systems are not in any way threatened by this problem?

(Mr Mountfield) I think it would be wrong for me to try to answer in detail on another Department's business. What I have asked the Ministry of Defence to do is to consider whether it is possible for them to disaggregate their return, at least to some extent, subject to requirements of security, so that we can have greater confidence about which parts are going to be on time and which are not. There are questions of concern over priority about it.

63. It would of course, as you are extremely well aware, be of extremely high public interest to know that that was the case.

(Mr Mountfield) Yes, of course.

64. I would certainly urge that whatever mechanisms to maintain the security should be taken into account so that we do have that reassurance in the same way as I would like the NHS to say that people are not going to die from a failure of the medical care in this country, and if there is any threat from any external forces that we can deliver our operational duties overseas.

(Mr Mountfield) Of course.

65. In a way the Report does not refer to the Department of Social Security who, from the Report,

[**Mr Hope** *Cont*]

appear to have got it right. What, in your view, was the key factor in the fact that the Department of Social Security have got it right?

(Mr Mountfield) First of all, I am glad that the Report is reassuring about the DSS and that does not surprise us because I think it confirms our own views, although they are not unique in that respect and there are others who have not been surveyed in quite this way which are equally up to speed. I think the key, as I see it as a non-IT specialist, is that they have followed very rigorous programme management. In other words, they have set out their objectives at the start of the various stages that have to be gone through and have made sure that they keep up to a programme to deal with that stage by stage.

66. Sir Alan, why did not you follow the DSS example?

(Sir Alan Langlands) Well, we have followed the same pattern. We are a very different sort of organisation, very heterogeneous compared to the DSS, but we do have very clear project management arrangements in place. We have been monitoring the Health Service on that basis. Our own project framework follows the usual so-called prince criteria and indeed the NAO Report, I think, does not challenge our project framework.

67. Yet in September 1996 you issued a letter from the Health Executive to authorities and trusts, but did not put any deadlines on it. There seemed to be a lack of specificity in there which might have meant that people got the letter and thought, "Yes, that is a problem we will deal with", but without any degree of urgency as a result of the failure to put specific deadlines for action.

(Sir Alan Langlands) Well, we did not follow through necessarily through monitoring, but we did follow through in a whole number of ways with some training events where the 400 key people from the Health Service were brought together in groups, and we followed through with some information packs that got a good response from the Health Service. We did actually monitor by the early part of 1997 on the basis of what health authorities and trusts had done as a result of that letter and the response was not as good as we wanted, which was one of the reasons we set up the monitoring process, but we do have some very good examples in the Health Service of people who worked to the guidance given in that letter and started the process off by the end of 1996 and that is showing dividends now.

68. So the dilemma that you faced was a poorer command structure—I cannot think of the words to use—and the DSS have got a more simplified, unified management system than that covering the NHS and that is the core reason for the lack of similar progress?

(Sir Alan Langlands) They certainly have a clearer command structure and, if you like, a more centralised approach to handling IT issues. I think it is fair to say that as the complexities and the difficulties that are arising around the year 2000 became clear, we moved much more into that mode than we naturally would.

69. I will come back, if I may, to Mr Mountfield. I am intrigued by the non-departmental public bodies.

Has any assessment been undertaken of the risks that they have, like the risks they have in the Health Service, from their failure to comply, whether it be security risks, health risks, safety risks? Has any assessment been done across the board of that?

(Mr Mountfield) I think the short answer is no, there has not yet been a comprehensive assessment in quite that form. I would expect local managers to have done very much that sort of thing as part of the ordinary processes of good management, but, as you know, this June return was the first time we have attempted to put comprehensive information together for the whole wider public sector and it is clear that we are not yet there and we have more work to do to fine-tune that analysis and make sure we have a comprehensive picture.

70. We are just guessing at what might go wrong really and I am wondering whether we should have a clearer idea from those non-departmental public bodies of their assessment of their own risks that they carry and how they are tackling them.

(Mr Mountfield) Well, as you will see from the material that was put on the Internet, there is some detail. It varies in quality and I think that has clearly got to be improved, but they are already under encouragement to publish as much information as possible either on the Internet or by holding public meetings, their ordinary management meetings in public, and that process ought to begin to raise questions about at least the more sensitive of the bodies concerned, but it covers a wide range and some of them, for example, advisory committees and so on, where frankly the IT risks are not all that great.

71. That is my dilemma. My dilemma is that I have no way of judging that. I have no way of knowing, but there could be a whole range of things which do not matter and there could be a number of things which really do matter and about which we appear not to have the information. Indeed in March of this year we established a new team of co-ordinators which you are running. Why did we not do that back in September 1996 when the DSS established their Project Management Board and the Health Executive sent out their letter of guidance? Why have we waited over a year and a half to do this for all these other areas where there could be as critical issues to health, safety and security?

(Mr Mountfield) Well, I do not think it is quite as inactive as that sounds. The process began about the middle of 1996 when the then Deputy Prime Minister asked colleagues to make sure that all the public bodies for which they were responsible set programmes in hand to correct the problem and that must include contingency planning of course, so I think there is quite a lot of evidence, bit by bit, that that has been done. What we have not had hitherto is a comprehensive picture across the whole wider public sector and we have got more to do to secure that.

72. I would agree that we have not got a comprehensive picture and we need it, but I also feel that there seems to be a different flavour of enthusiasm between a government minister encouraging colleagues to ask these questions and a department

[Mr Hope *Cont*]

setting up a project board to actively intervene and manage, and I was wondering why we have waited this long before we have actively intervened and managed.

(Mr Mountfield) I think that reflects the different constitutional position that ministers can have the power to direct their departments to do things, but they do not have the power to direct elected bodies, like local authorities, or statutory bodies who have been appointed by due process. What they can do clearly is try and encourage departments to gather information, to press authorities to take it into account, and to encourage bodies to publicise as much information as possible.

73. I just think there is a difference, not constitutionally, but in a sense of urgency and that whilst this probably emerged in 1995, most people got it in 1996 and it appears that for the rest of the public sector, they had not got on to it until 1998 which is literally two years before the problem actually happens. Indeed it could be before then for some systems. This is not a constitutional problem, more a problem of really grasping it and taking it seriously.

(Mr Mountfield) It depends what you mean by grasping it. If you mean the collection of quarterly returns then, yes, I acknowledge that has only just started. Of course, the purpose of collecting returns is not to initiate action that has not taken place but rather to check that it is already in hand. I think there is plenty of evidence that bodies right through the public sector have done a great deal already. Many of them may be ahead of Central Government for all we know.

74. For all we know.

(Mr Mountfield) For all we know.

75. I would like to pick up a point Mr Leslie made about recovering costs. Did I hear you right to say that you are taking specific action to look at potential recovery costs from suppliers of software and hardware?

(Mr Mountfield) No, not quite in those terms. The question of recovery will depend on the individual contract or the individual procurement.

76. Are you taking action on these specific contracts of individual procurement to see the possibility?

(Mr Mountfield) No, that is for individual departments to do. The priority must be to make sure that as much equipment and systems are compliant as possible. The question of picking up the pieces afterwards if they go wrong is a second order question. It is a very important one and departments will be doing that to the extent that it is possible to change the position that is already contractually committed.

77. When you say it is up to departments to do, does that mean that you are not giving central guidance to departments, you are not going to be encouraging them objectively and getting them to pursue the £400 million we appear to be spending? Does that mean you are not doing that?

(Mr Mountfield) There is a certain amount one can do centrally. I think the point about liability questions is that one can only judge it in the circumstances of the individual contract or procurement. One can give

general guidance on liability questions but all the advice we have so far, and the NHS have got some particular advice in preparation for their circumstances is that, it has to be applied to the individual case.

78. I would quite like to see the guidance you have issued.

(Mr Mountfield) We have not issued guidance in that form. We have made some inquiries of the lawyers. The advice, as I have said, is you can set up general lines but you cannot say very much more than that without putting the individual case.

79. You have not issued guidance?

(Mr Mountfield) No.

80. Do you think there is a need to issue guidance given the point Mr Leslie has raised about the potential liability that these organisations supplying the software and hardware could carry?

(Mr Mountfield) It is a matter we are looking at at the moment but we have not yet taken the decision to issue guidance in those terms. Perhaps I am misleading you, it has been pointed out to me that the general question is addressed in the very substantial six volume guidance the CCTA has published. That covers a huge range of different year 2000 issues. There is material there but we have not issued a specific guidance letter on liability questions up to now.

Mr Hope: My time is up but I share Mr Leslie's concern that you have been taken for a ride and that the people that supply materials known to be defective, which I regard them as being, should be pursued for doing so. I think that is part of the Government's responsibility in this case.

Mr Clifton-Brown

81. Good afternoon. Can I ask you, Mr Mountfield, about the 9.9.99 problem. A senior air traffic controller advised me not to travel in an aircraft on 9 September next year, 1999, the four nine problem, because a lot of the older IT equipment may well cease to function on that day or if not that day the day after. Is this a problem the Government has addressed because it is considerably earlier than the year 2000 problem we have been looking at so far?

(Mr Mountfield) If I may I will ask Mr Gladwyn to help us on that. My understanding is that there is quite a number of caution dates of which 9.9.99 is one, and the year 2000 is another. Of course we are already living with this problem in some cases. Computer systems in the private sector as well as the public sector are already throwing up peculiarities geared to one of those caution dates. That really reinforces the need to get on with the job and do it as soon as possible.

(Mr Gladwyn) Specifically on the 9.9.99 problem it is in fact in the CCTA guidance which was published as one of the questions the department should look out for. I recall from my days as an ICL on 1900 programmer, that in those days 9.9.99 was used to stop the machine so it would be interesting if such a code was still in use. I think it is a very important problem. I think that whilst of course people should be prudent about their travel arrangements, I would hope that the

[Mr Clifton-Brown *Cont]*

air traffic control systems have this taken into account and checked and corrected.

82.   It is not only a problem for air traffic control, it could be equally as important a problem in any field, the NHS or any other field the Government covers. What specific measures, other than merely putting it in page goodness knows what in the guidance, is the Government actually doing about it?

(Mr Gladwyn)   It is part of the checking and testing programme for year 2000 compliance which will be required for a department to make a statement that its systems will be year 2000 compliant.

83.   Can I move on to all of the gentlemen and try and get a little bit of a better handle on these costs. Can I start with you, Sir Alan, and congratulations, as others have also congratulated you. You have given the Committee this afternoon a figure of £320 million as a figure for the NHS. I take it that is made up of £170 million for compliance, the millennium compliance, plus £150 million for upgrading clinical and IT equipment and other equipment, is that correct?

(Sir Alan Langlands)   No, it is made up of £170 million to deal with all of the IT issues and £150 million as a contingency against problems with medical devices.

84.   Can I confirm that figure is for the whole of the NHS, i.e. England, Wales, Scotland and Northern Ireland?

(Sir Alan Langlands)   No, that figure is for the NHS in England, which is my responsibility.

85.   Could you or could Mr Mountfield give us the entire NHS figure?

(Mr Mountfield)   No, I do not think I can give you a figure for the Welsh, Scottish and Northern Irish figures. Those I do not think will be included within the £400 million we have for Central Government because in those territories, as in England, they are treated as separate categories. That is one of the areas we have not got mapped at a central level.

86.   Mr Mountfield, presumably you advised the Prime Minister when he made his speech on 30 March in which he said that the overall figure for Central Government—paragraph 132, page 18—was likely to be in the order of three billion. How could you have arrived at that aggregate figure if you cannot tell the Committee this afternoon what the total figure for the NHS is?

(Mr Mountfield)   The three billion in the Prime Minister's speech was explicitly not a forecast by the Prime Minister. He said it was a figure he merely quoted and it seemed to him reasonable. The calculation that I tried to describe a few moments ago was that we have certain reasonably firm figures for substantial parts of the public sector. We have £400 million or so for Central Government and the armed forces. We have a figure which may be a rather rough and ready figure, £500 million for local government, and we have a figure of up to about £320 million for the NHS in England. There is then a series of other parts of the wider public sector which lead us to the view that about three billion will not be unreasonable. There is another way of looking at this problem which

is to start from the assumption that £400 million we have got for Central Government is about right, and clearly that can be no more than an assumption at this stage, and that relates to something like 700,000 employees in the Civil Service and in the armed services, which is about 13 or 14 per cent of public sector employment. On a rule of thumb basis that indicates that three billion may well be the order of magnitude.

87.   I am getting very worried about this figure. I am going to ask the Treasury how this figure is going to be financed and then I am going to ask the National Audit Office whether they think the figure is robust. Can I ask the Treasury, this is a substantial amount of money, £3 billion pounds, is it already provided for in the departmental budgets in the Red Book or is it to come out of the contingency reserve or will there be supplementary estimates?

(Mr Martin)   No, the Government's approach is that the costs should be met from within existing budgets but I would like to emphasise that not all of that three billion or any of the figures being quoted will be an additional call on resources. I think both witnesses have said that a lot of the year 2000 activity which is going on will involve for example the replacement of hardware and software which will have been a requirement in any event. Similarly, a lot of the cost will be of IT staff within the department who, when they are spending their time on year 2000 problems of course will be moved from other IT activities. So again these staff costs will not be an addition to total planned spending on IT by the department. That said, the Government's approach is that these costs should be met within existing plans.

88.   That is an extremely helpful answer because I want to come back to Mr Mountfield in a minute about how far the Government's IT programme has been delayed by this. Can I ask you, Deputy C&AG, you have in your Report this figure of £3 billion and you also have in your Report paragraph 16, page 8 which says that the costs to the NHS alone could vary between £200 and £850 million. Now, if the costs as a whole for government go up towards the top end of your estimates, we are way above the £3 billion figure that the Prime Minister estimates. Have you done any work to try and ascertain how robust this £3 billion figure is?

(Mr Le Marechal)   No. As Mr Mountfield said, the Report does not say that it is the Prime Minister's own estimate, as it were. He commented that that ball-park figure was a reasonable one. Our Report draws attention to a great many things which now need to be addressed and, therefore, a great many uncertainties about any estimate which could be produced at this stage, so we have not found it appropriate at this stage to try and produce something which is more robust than £3 billion, but it is clear from our Report that there is a great deal of approximation and roughness attached to that figure.

89.   Well, given that it is a substantial figure, I wonder, Chairman, whether it would be reasonable to ask for a note from the Deputy C&AG as to how the £3 billion is broken down between government departments. Would that be feasible?

[Mr Clifton-Brown *Cont]*

(Mr Le Marechal) We will certainly try to get an analysis like that[1], Mr Clifton-Brown, but I do not think it was our figure either. It was not actually an analysis that we have produced.

90. If I can come back to you, Mr Mountfield, we have had several hearings in this Committee, not least the one with Sir Alan Langlands on Read Codes, of severe problems with IT programmes within government. We heard that the NIRS 2 system, for example, in the Contributions Agency was likely to lead to employers not being given their appropriate rebates on time at the beginning of the financial tax year. Now, they are very, very serious problems. How far, in your view, is this effort and financial cost of the compliance problem delaying the entire Government's updating of IT systems?

(Mr Mountfield) First of all, may I narrow the question down initially at least to the central government figure of £400 million? As I have tried to explain, that £400 million is made up of estimates made by operational professionals right through the central government machine who are already part-way through the programme. I cannot guarantee that that number will not escalate because clearly there is a long history of escalation, but I think as we get nearer towards completion, one has an increasing amount of confidence that that is of the right order, though it may be a little on the low side, it may not. Now, that figure is actually quite small in relation to total running costs.

91. With respect, Mr Mountfield, I have moved on from figures and I asked you in relation to the Government's IT programme and the severe problems, with NIRS 2 and Read Codes being just two of them, how far the devotion of this huge amount of financial resources and human resources was going to delay the development of the Government's total IT programme? I will come to Sir Alan in a minute, but *Computing* magazine estimates that in the NHS alone it will be two years, so can you tell us across the government spectrum how much it will be?

(Mr Mountfield) No, I do not think I can in those terms. The Government of course does not run its IT programme as a single unitary programme; it is operationally, and quite rightly, integrated with business plans right through every department and agency and it is much more sensible, I think, to look at it from the point of view of how it fits into each department's programme. As a very rough order of magnitude because there is no budgeting calculated on this basis, the Government spends at least £2 billion a year on IT procurement and services, upgrading and so on, so a figure of £400 million over two or three financial years is not hugely disproportionate. It clearly changed some priorities within those programmes. It may mean, for example, in some cases accelerating replacement, which is justified for good reasons otherwise. It may mean postponing an upgrade in some cases. I do not think we have, indeed I think it is unlikely that we could ever get, a comprehensive view or assessment of the extent to which priorities are being displaced, but we get no sign

from the reports we have got that that is becoming a major worry to the departments.

92. Sir Alan, I will, you will be glad to know, move you off figures and on to one or two specific items. The Report makes quite clear that the individual chief executives of the trusts and the health authorities are responsible directly to you for compliance and that they are responsible for compliance in each of their areas. Why is it that the Medical Devices Agency is not ensuring compliance of a class of equipment across the entire country? That would seem to me to make a far greater degree of sense.

(Sir Alan Langlands) Well, just for the record, not to duck the question, but for the record, the Medical Devices Agency is not accountable to the NHS Executive, but its accountability is to another part of the Department of Health, but of course we are working closely with them. I think the point is that it is impossible, in dealing with this sort of huge range of equipment that we have to deal with, to generalise even for each class of equipment. This is a global market and there are literally thousands of different items of equipment in play and to ensure or to check compliance, you have to be clear about manufacturer, you have to be clear about the function of the equipment, the model of the equipment, sometimes even the batch number, and bits of equipment with the same batch number might even have different embedded chips in them, so the agreement that we reached with the Medical Devices Agency is that the initial check on each bit of equipment would be made by the appropriate person holding that equipment in the Health Service and the manufacturer. If there were difficulties, however, in getting information back or, as we built up our knowledge, there was a responsibility to disseminate that information, that then would be something that the Medical Devices Agency would carry out on our behalf.

93. Surely there must be huge amounts of duplication going on with each trust, each health authority with the same bit of equipment as another trust and another health authority going to the manufacturer and doing the same compliance audit. Would it not make sense for the Medical Devices Agency to take over a class of equipment and in that way it is far more likely that where there are problems, a central government agency would pick them up? If one trust has one problem with one bit of his equipment, it may well not be picked up.

(Sir Alan Langlands) It is not the case that checking one piece of equipment necessarily means year 2000 compliance for a very similar piece of equipment. The point is that each of these things has to be checked individually and there has to be a plan and each health authority and each trust has a great inventory of all the different bits and classes of equipment that they use. Now, clearly there are well-established partnership relationships between the Medical Devices Agency and the NHS and clearly, as we have built up our information, we have established in a central unit a clearing house, a database on which people can exchange information and indeed

---

[1] *Note:* See Evidence, Appendix 1, page 18 (PAC 367).

[Mr Clifton-Brown *Cont]*

manufacturers are being very good sometimes at exchanging information with us.

94. What problems have already arisen in the NHS? We hear, for example, that University College are not able to take outpatient appointments after the year 2000. Are you aware that problems are already starting because of this non-compliance of IT systems?

(Sir Alan Langlands) We are certainly aware of the potential problems that I referred to in relation to the call and recall systems with screening and we are certainly aware of potential problems, which have now been dealt with, in relation to prescribing for people with chronic diseases. We are aware of some operational problems where instead of entering a two-digit code, OO, to represent the year 2000, there is now a requirement on staff to enter a four-digit code. All of these problems, as they arise, are being systematically dealt with by the project managers in each trust and often, as I have underlined in the previous answer, working in partnership with the manufacturers and the suppliers because they are not on the whole in a competitive relationship, but they are there and they are keen to work with us on these issues.

95. Final question for you, Sir Alan. On paragraph 2.58, page 43—I have two yellow cards so I suppose that must amount to a red card—the NAO recommends further selective direct intervention. Are you proposing any further selective direct intervention?

(Sir Alan Langlands) Yes. The regional offices are already intervening on the basis of the March 1998 returns and that will continue. Intervention can be, if you like, aimed at bringing people up to speed, it can also be aimed at helping people, supporting people, by disseminating information on both strands we are using on this issue.

96. A final question, going back to Mr Hope's question, can you say to the Committee, sitting here as confidently as you can, you do not think anybody will die directly as a result of these problems?

(Sir Alan Langlands) I am saying that we have systematically assessed all the risks and will continue to do so. We will continue to deal with them as systematically as we can between now and the end of December 1999. Of course I cannot guarantee a yes response to your question, I do not think you would expect me to.

Mr Williams

97. Mr Mountfield, did I hear you correctly, did you say the cost you now estimate to Central Government is £402 million?

(Mr Mountfield) Yes.

98. The NAO tells us that between November of last year and March of this year the costs rose six per cent to £393 million. That is an increase of £23 million. You are now telling us that since March of this year to the beginning of this month it has gone up another nine million pounds?

(Mr Mountfield) Yes.

99. So in six months it has risen £32 million. So the rate of increase at the moment is £64 million on an annualised basis?

(Mr Mountfield) Yes, that sounds about right.

100. It does. It does not sound good but it sounds right. Any reason to think that is the end of it?

(Mr Mountfield) No, I do not think it would be prudent to say that with the record of forecasting in the IT field one could be absolutely confident it is not going to increase. All I would say is that as we get deeper into this programme professionals are looking in detail at the forward costs. In some cases they are reducing them. In a few cases they are increasing them. The overall effect, as you rightly point out, is that it is still increasing. I would be frankly surprised if it did not go on increasing a little bit.

101. If it did increase at the same rate between now and the year 2000 there would be an extra £180 million on costs.

(Mr Mountfield) I think it is unlikely to be at that rate, if only because the proportion of work still undone is reducing all the time. We have already spent, we believe, at least a quarter of the total.

102. Can I ask you a bit about defence. We are told that defence is the area which is having difficulty. In what sense is it having difficulty and in what way is it affected?

(Mr Mountfield) I do not think I meant to imply that they were having general difficulty.

103. The NAO report refers to them having difficulty.

(Mr Mountfield) The point I tried to make was in the area of skilled resources, which is drawn attention to, I think, in the NAO report, it has certainly been mentioned in the Chancellor of the Duchy's statements, and the problem there is not that they are finding it impossible to get the skilled resources but they are having to divert them from other IT activities. This is an example of where tackling the year 2000 problem is leading to postponement of other activities.

104. That applies to Sir Alan Langlands as well does it not?

(Mr Mountfield) To some extent.

105. Why single out the Ministry of Defence as being particularly vulnerable?

(Mr Mountfield) Because the majority of departments have said that they are not finding that skill shortage is a problem. It may be that there are financial reasons why they are having to divert from other matters into year 2000 work but in the Ministry of Defence's case they say they are concerned about skill supply shortage.

106. Defence now is very IT based, is it not?

(Mr Mountfield) Indeed.

107. Is there any strategic or operational risk as a result of this worry about skills?

(Mr Mountfield) I do not think I could competently answer on that point. The general messages are reassuring on that point but you would

[Mr Williams *Cont]*

not expect me, I am sure, to answer on the Ministry of Defence's detailed security consideration.

108.   No, but I want to know about it.
(Mr Mountfield) Indeed.

109.   Would you please put a written report in[1] because I think if there is anything wrong on the defence front the Committee and perhaps the Defence Select Committee would want to know about it.
(Mr Mountfield) Indeed.

110.   We will alert our sister Committee to that fact. Would you let us have an urgent note on that?
(Mr Mountfield) Yes, we will.

111.   Thank you. Sir Alan, again may I congratulate you on your elevation.
(Sir Alan Langlands) Thank you.

112.   Your's has been a miserable job, we well understand that.
(Sir Alan Langlands) Thank you very much.

113.   This Committee has not done much to make it much happier I realise.
(Sir Alan Langlands) I suspect I am about to see the golden goal, Chairman.

114.   I am in an amicable mood I promise you. Tell me, our old friends RISP and HISP, Wessex Regional Information System and your own national hospital information system which cost £100 million to save three million pounds a year—great investment—how are they affected by the millennium bug, if at all?
(Sir Alan Langlands) They are affected in the same way as all our major operating systems. We have talked a lot tonight about medical equipment but, of course, we do have other so-called patient administration systems as a class of systems in the Health Service and these are affected. These changes and the necessary checks and compliance checks on these systems have been worked through with the manufacturers as it has in relation to all our equipment.

115.   On HISP it is not long ago we were looking at that. It is a fairly recent project, is it not, the national hospital information system This was at the frontiers of application of information technology to your sector of Government service. It was preparing us for the next century. Are you telling us they overlooked the fact that the next century has a different date?
(Sir Alan Langlands) No, I think it does go back some time, Chairman. These systems have been developing right through from the late 1980s, through the early 1990s and into the mid 1990s.

116.   What is your estimate of the cost of those two particular projects which as a Committee we know a fair amount about?
(Sir Alan Langlands) I cannot break down the costs that I quoted by system. The breakdown I have here is in relation to the different sorts of trusts.

117.   That is not trusts, is it, you run that?
(Sir Alan Langlands) No, no.

118.   Who runs HISP?
(Sir Alan Langlands) The HISS system or further developments of that system are run in individual trusts as part of their normal activities.

119.   It is a national integrated system? Does that not bring it within your remit?
(Sir Alan Langlands) It is not a national integrated system.

120.   It was meant to be a national integrated system when 100 million was spent. That is another piece of good news for us.
(Sir Alan Langlands) Chairman, if it would help, I do have my expert with me. He might want to talk about that.
(Mr Burns) You mentioned two systems, you mentioned the RISP system which was a regional system which was actually abandoned at the time.

121.   It was abandoned, they were using a residual basis, using some of the systems within.
(Mr Burns) The regionally integrated system was abandoned. There are some regionally integrated patient administration systems that are provided by a variety of suppliers.

122.   Forget that and go on to the national one.
(Mr Burns) All of these patient administration systems are being actively investigated in conjunction with suppliers and we expect all of them to be resolved in terms of year 2000 compliance problems by the dates that we have set.

123.   That is good news but at what cost?
(Mr Burns) In many cases the costs will be covered as part of the contract with the suppliers. I have not got individual costs in terms of the costs falling on specific hospitals. They are part of the general costs.

124.   Is it possible going back to your office you might be able—I do not mean this in any unpleasant sense—to do us a note in relation to that?
(Mr Burns) Yes[2]. If you are alluding specifically to the hospital information systems that were the subject of the previous PAC report we could let you have a note of what specific costs for year 2000 compliance arise.

125.   All we want is the information.
(Sir Alan Langlands) Yes.

126.   Sir Alan, I know you cannot say this because as a civil servant you dare not but it must be a matter of some concern that all these costs are having to be absorbed within existing budgets when some people are not living within their existing budget.
(Sir Alan Langlands) Well, I think when the Committee sees the accounts for the Health Service, which are not published yet, for the last financial year, you will see a very significant improvement in issues of budgetary control and the scale of the deficit has reduced very substantially indeed.

127.   You are not suggesting that there are going to be trusts who will not be in deficit?

---

[1]   *Note:* See Evidence, Appendix 3, page 20 (PAC 360).

[2]   *Note:* See Evidence, Appendix 2, page 19 (PAC 344).

[Mr Williams *Cont]*

(Sir Alan Langlands) No, I am not suggesting that at all.

128. So what happens to them and what happens to the people who are dependent on them?

(Sir Alan Langlands) Well, where people are in deficit, in terms of the Committee's and the NAO's definition of "deficit", there will be a recurring deficit. They will be in a deficit position, if you like, in relation to their year-on-year budgets.

129. Are you trying to say that they will be in bigger deficit?

(Sir Alan Langlands) No, I am not saying that at all. I was going on to say that where these trusts are in deficit, there is either in place an action plan to reduce that deficit or there is a special dispensation approved by ministers to carry that deficit forward and there are often very good reasons why a deficit will arise.

130. All we want to know, and this is what we are concerned about, is that every trust, regardless of whether it is in deficit or not, is going to be able to conform to the requirements for the millennium change without the possible extra loss of service to its patients.

(Sir Alan Langlands) The money will be allocated on a non-recurring basis to deal with the millennium issue. The lion's share of the expenditure, £210 million of the £320 million, will be spent this year. I think that sum is insulated from the routine of Health Service spending and I do not think that the expenditure of that sum will lead to any downgrading of patient care.

131. What about the activities of the Medical Devices Agency? They seemed to wake up to this problem very, very late, did they not? In fact they were issuing quite sanguine reports when you later came along and issued warnings that if there was not compliance, there could be trouble, putting patients' health at risk and lives at risk.

(Sir Alan Langlands) They did produce early reports in 1996. I think you are right to suggest that it has taken some time for the whole question of embedded chips of electro-medical equipment to perhaps be given the same emphasis that has been given to IT systems, which, as we have said earlier, have been running since 1995/96, but I am sure, absolutely sure now that the Medical Devices Agency and the NHS Executive are working hand in glove on this issue and that the Medical Devices Agency are providing proper support to the NHS.

132. So coming back to the point the Chairman raised right at the outset of the 10 per cent of trusts who are not confident of fixing their systems and the 15 per cent who are not confident of fixing their medical equipment, how have you singled these out for administrative supervision over this period? Have you done anything special in relation to those to try to bring them up into phase with everyone else?

(Sir Alan Langlands) I think as a generality that the position has improved from the NAO study period which was September/October 1997 and the position that we monitored and recorded for every trust——

133. What would you make it now? What would the 10 per cent and the 15 per cent be now then?

(Sir Alan Langlands) In terms of?

134. Well, it was 10 per cent of trusts who are not confident of fixing their systems, so what per cent would you say now?

(Sir Alan Langlands) I think all trusts have now accepted that they have to meet the——

135. No, no, that is not the question. The question is about the fact that they are not confident, but you said that they understand that they have to, but that does not mean they are confident of meeting it, does it?

(Sir Alan Langlands) I am assured——

136. You can tell the England team that it has to go out and win, but there is someone else on the field as well. It is not entirely within their control, is it? Just for you to say that they have been told is not good enough and it does not mean it gets done.

(Sir Alan Langlands) All the returns we have, the March 1998 returns, and we will see the June returns just in a few weeks' time, suggest that the two deadlines that I outlined at the beginning to the Chairman will be met across the NHS.

137. That is so but you are saying that ten per cent who were not confident of fixing their systems are now confident?

(Sir Alan Langlands) That I believe to be true. I think everyone will meet the targets that have been set.

138. So that is confidence there. And the 15 per cent who were not confident of fixing their medical equipment, you think they are now confident?

(Sir Alan Langlands) I do not think they are necessarily always confident of fixing their medical equipment and that is one of the reasons that £150 million has been set aside by the NHS as a contingency sum.

139. Why is the equipment giving so much trouble when the specialist organisation, the Medical Devices Agency, had indicated there was not a great problem?

(Sir Alan Langlands) First and foremost we do not know if it is giving trouble. There are problems in some places that seem to have been adequately resolved in the relationship between the NHS and the Medical Devices Agency that I described. There are some pieces of equipment that are so critical and cannot be tested in the time frame that they might have to be replaced or have parts renewed. That is why the £150 million has been set aside as a contingency sum.

140. What, to buy new equipment?

(Sir Alan Langlands) Sorry?

141. To buy replacement equipment?

(Sir Alan Langlands) To buy replacement equipment. I said earlier we spend on that heading of medical surgical supplies and equipment nearly a billion pounds a year in the Health Service, often to buy new equipment by drawing it forward if you like from its natural time cycle, in other words bringing it forward, say, from 2003 to——

142. Writing it off early?

[Mr Williams *Cont*]

(Sir Alan Langlands) No, no. Perhaps in the case of a piece of equipment that may be eight or nine years old and due for replacement in 2002 or 2003, bringing it forward to 1999 to be absolutely clear that compliance is achieved.

143. In the last resort you assure us that is what you will do?

(Sir Alan Langlands) That is what trusts and health authorities and others have been asked to do, the money has been set aside for that purpose.

144. Can I ask you one personal question. Are you due for retirement before or after the year 2000?

(Sir Alan Langlands) I hope that I will be here in the year 2000 to answer to the Committee but, of course, that will not be my decision.

145. I look forward to seeing you in the first PAC after 1 January 2000.

(Sir Alan Langlands) I will make a date.

Chairman

146. Thank you, gentlemen. My two questions that I was going to ask have been, as I suspected, picked up in general questions. I will actually extend Mr Williams' questioning to you, Mr Mountfield. When we have the February 2000 PAC, the sweep up, mop up, or whatever it is, will you be with us? I notice you were born in 1939?

(Mr Mountfield) No, I shall not, I shall be retired by then.

147. So whoever takes over from you will be appearing in that Committee. It is a problem we have had before with accounting officers. A last question to the Treasury before we wrap up. It has become very apparent that the costs are going to escalate on a number of fronts on this. You gave a very smooth answer, if I may describe it in that way, to Mr Clifton-Brown. I want it put clearly on the record, what you are saying is—yes or no will answer this—Treasury policy is these costs will be absorbed by the Department irrespective of how difficult the problem, irrespective of existing ITCL, irrespective of available staff capable of transfer, irrespective of the types of budget and irrespective of how dangerous trailing will be?

(Mr Martin) I do not think, Chairman, I said anything like that at all. The Government's current policy is that the costs as they have so far been identified should be met from within existing plans. I am fairly confident that neither this nor any other Government is actually going to allow a situation to arise where compliance could not be achieved because of financial constraints of some sort. I am quite sure that if Mr Mountfield in the departmental returns were to identify that there was a cost increase that could not be absorbed he would bring it to the attention of the Treasury and the Treasury would react sensibly to that.

Chairman: There you are, Mr Mountfield, a helpful PAC meeting for you. Can I just say to you and to Sir Alan, thank you for your time, it is a very important question. Thank you.

APPENDIX 1

MANAGING THE MILLENNIUM THREAT (PAC 97–98/367)

Supplementary Memorandum submitted by the Comptroller and Auditor General, National Audit Office

Q89. *The derivation of the £3 billion estimate for remedial work across all the public sector*

The *Committee* asked for details of how the estimate of £3 billion for remedial work across the public sector had been arrived at.

The reference in the C&AG's report (paragraphs 5 and 1.32) to £3 billion was a report of the speech given by the Prime Minister to the Action 2000 Midland Bank Conference on 30 March 1998.

The *Accounting Officer of the Public Service (OPS)*, Robin Mountfield, said the £3 billion figure in the Prime Minister's 30 March speech was explicitly not forecast by the Prime Minster, but rather a figure others had used which the Prime Minister had thought was reasonable. The Prime Minister himself referred to the origin of the £3 billion figure in response to a written question in the Commons on 30 April:

> "The figure of up to £3 billion for the cost of millennium compliance across the public sector was an estimate to indicate the possible scale of the problem which is faced by the sector. It took account of forecasts which have been made by independent experts and companies with experience of dealing with the costs of tackling this problem. Such forecasts have ranged from £1 billion to £3 billion. These forecasts are within a range because of the actual costs of compliance are not easy to predict accurately in advance and historically have tended to be underestimated."

(Written Answer to Malcolm Bruce MP 30 April, Official Report, column 173–4).

Following on from this in his evidence to the Committee Mr Mountfield described two routes to support a very broad estimate of that order:

    (i) figures had been given for central government of £402 million in the Chancellor of the Duchy's statement), for local government of £500 million (by the Local Government Association) and of

£170–£320 million for the NHS. Those excluded other parts of the wider public such as TECs; Higher and Further Education; BBC; NDPBs; London Underground; Post Office; etc. Making allowance for these and other public sector bodies, a figure of £3 billion looked plausible.

(ii) Alternatively a crude calculation could be based on an extrapolation from the central governments estimate of £402 million for approaching 700,000 employees (Civil Service and Armed Forces), an average of around £600 per employee. For a public sector as a whole employing just over 5 million people (see Economic Trends, March 1995), if the same cost per employee applied, this extrapolation suggested a total of around £3 billion. This calculation was, of course, based on extremely broad assumptions and had no pretentions to be forecast.

National Audit Office

14 July 1998

APPENDIX 2

MANAGING THE MILLENNIUM THREAT (PAC 97–98/344)

Supplementary Memorandum submitted by NHS Executive

Question 124. *Hospital Information Support Systems (HISS) initiative and Year 2000 compliance*

The Committee asked for details of the costs associated with year 2000 compliance for the Hospital Information Support Systems (HISS) initiative.

Of the nine HISS sites examined by the National Audit Office, seven have entered into maintenance agreements with their system suppliers. In all of these cases, the supplier's costs associated with making the systems Year 2000 complaint are covered within these existing maintenance agreements.

The sites in this category are:

Darlington Memorial Hospital NHS Trust (Supplier: MDIS)

Greenwich Healthcare NHS Trust (Supplier: HBOC)

Kidderminster Healthcare NHS Trust (Supplier: HBOC)

Addenbrooke's NHS Trust (Supplier: MDIS)

Norfolk and Norwich Health Care NHS Trust (Supplier: MDIS)

James Paget Hospital NHS Trust (Supplier: MDIS)

West Suffolk Hospitals NHS Trust (Supplier: MDIS)

Nottingham City Hospital NHS Trust (Supplier: Oracle) is responsible for the maintenance of its own system application and in this instance the costs are estimated at £61,000.

Birmingham Heartlands Hospital NHS Trust (Supplier: IBM/GTE) has no existing maintenance agreement following the withdrawal of the application software supplier from the UK healthcare market. This site is therefore responsible for the costs associated with making the system Year 2000 compliant which are estimated at £501,000.

NHS Executive

30 June 1998

APPENDIX 3

MILLENNIUM DATE CHANGE: IMPLICATION FOR STRATEGIC DEFENCES (PAC 97–98/360)

Supplementary Memorandum submitted by the Office of Public Service

MoD is embarked on major "Year 2000" Programme, costing around £200 million and involving over 700 staff.

To date some 20,000 date-dependent systems have been identified. This embraces a very broad spectrum of systems, performing a wide range of functions (from standard desk-top PCs to micro-processor chips embedded in complex weapon systems.

Of the systems so far identified for remedial *action*, priority is being given to those which are critical to maintaining the operational effectiveness of the Armed Forces. Within this category, the *very highest* importance is being attached to systems underpinning the effectiveness, security and safety of the strategic nuclear deterrent.

We are confident that all key operationally critical systems, including those relating to strategic defences, will be rectified before problems are encountered. Progress is reviewed regularly to ensure that new problems are identified and resolved at an early stage.

As a further precaution, however, separate *contingency plans* are being drawn up to ensure that we can maintain our commitments and operational readiness even if we do experience unexpected Year 2000-related equipment failures, or if key suppliers are prevented from meeting their contracted delivery schedule.

Office of Public Service

1 July 1998

Printed in the United Kingdom by The Stationery Office Limited
8/98   384166   19585   CRC Supplied

ISBN 0-10-555001-9

9 780105 550013